Untold History Of America

Let The Truth Be Known

Copyright © 2009
by
David E. Robinson

All Rights Reserved
Parts of this book may be reproduced subject to due and specific acknowledgment of their source.

MAINE-PATRIOT.com
3 Linnell Circle
Brunswick, Maine 04011

maine-patriot.com

A wise man will hear, and will increase learning. — *Proverbs 1:5.*

Surely in vain the net is spread in the sight of any bird. — Proverbs 1:17.

Untold History Of America

Let The Truth Be Known

Contents

	Introduction ---------------------------------	9
1	The British Board of Trade -----------------	11
2	Emergency War Powers --------------------	17
3	Povincial Congress -------------------------	21
4	Your Joint Venture -------------------------	25
5	The King's Legisature Still Rules ----------	29
6	Are You Supreme In The Scheme Of Things? -------------------------------	35
7	The Connection ---------------------------	37
8	Protection Of The King's Interest In America -----------------------------------	43
9	We Are Still The Enemy ---------------------	47
10	Commerce Rules Over Freedom ---------	57
11	The Masses ---------------------------------	63
12	What Will It Take To Become Free? ------	67
13	How Many Really Care? -------------------	71
14	Natural Law Is The Way To Go ------------	75
15	Your Consent -------------------------------	79
16	Merge With The Modern Times ----------	87
17	Hello Citizen - Good Bye Natural Rights ---------------------------------------	99

18 Legal Plunder Is The Law ------------------ 103
19 Meaning Of A Real Christian -------------- 109
20 Foreign Bankers join Domestic
       Conspirators ------------------------------- 115
21 We Cannot Charge Treason -------------- 119
22 Political or Legal Terminology --------------121
23 Judicial Verbicide ----------------------------- 133
24 Lost Logic & Common Sense ------------- 139
25 Redress, What Is That? --------------------- 143
26 What Other Authors Say ------------------- 149
27 Finally Making Sense -------------------------159
28 A Closing Note ------------------------------- 167
29 What You Don't Know -----------------------171
30 The Dollar's Demise ------------------------- 173
     Breaking News -------------------------------- 187
     Epilogue --------------------------------------- 195
            Appendix

Let The Truth Be Known   7

Introduction

Contrary to what many believe, the American people have never been free from enslavement to other men, despite the writings of the Declaration of Independence and the Constitutions of the United States and the States.

The purpose of this book is to bring forth the basic groundwork of the state of affairs that people prior to us have allowed to take place. It exposes all the lies about the Constitutions of the United States and the States being created by the people. All other issues of the patriot movement today are collateral, as are the war power acts of Lincoln and Roosevelt; birth certificates; zip codes; social security; and other issues that you might think important today.

Not that they are *not* important, they are, but this doesn't matter. What only matters is how these issues got to this stage.

Argue any of these issues — as has been done in the past — and you place yourself under *the presumption* that you are one of their "citizens" — an "individual" or "resident"; and your history.

You must realize what you're up against today.

We are thrown into a chess game without any knowledge of the rules, and how the game began, and how it is run.

The establishment relies on us *fighting* them on *their* issues, issues that amount to *nothing* in the game.

It becomes a lose, lose situation.

They keep moving their queen around, taking all our chess pieces, no matter what we do. A *few* of us might escape, here and there, but that's a small amount, compared to the whole. This book shows you the groundwork and the rules by which the game is played.

Let The Truth Be Known

The corporate state was already formed at the very beginning of this country's life.

By 1791, the federal government had *already* organized the Bank of the United States — *a privately owned corporation,* — and by 1816, corporations were again threatening the vision of the Framers.

The Santa Ana case marked the demise of a nation of men, and the coronation of a new kind of nation, *the corporate state.* And the 14th Amendment soon became the formidable weapon used to subject *both* the blacks *and* the whites to the will of corporate America.

After reviewing this book you will recognize the *fascism* we are under today.

1
The British Board of Trade

Charles I granted the "Carolina" — part of what is now Virginia, North and South Carolina, and Georgia — to Sir Robert Heath, in 1629. He then transferred the "Carolina" territory to Henry Fredrick Heart (Lord Maltrave) in 1638. In 1663, Charles II replaced Heart's grant by granting the "Carolina" to eight men called Proprietors, who began the first land tax called a *quitrent*. This tax quit the landowners from certain (not all) feudal obligations to the Crown. This money went to the Proprietors to run the English colony, and the remainder went to the king.

The Proprietors created a document called "Concessions & Agreement," in 1665. This was really the first constitution, established to entice newcomers to settle in "Carolina."

The British Board of Trade

In 1669, the Proprietors created the "Constitutions of Carolina" allegedly written by John Locke who served as secretary to the Proprietors. In this position, Locke was true to the Crown, but did he espouse freedom? This Constitution provided for a Feudal System.

His plan for the government consisted of an executive and legislative branch and completely ignored the judiciary. This constitution he helped to draft created the countries and the holders of nobility to operate them.

The Proprietors chose a Governor of North Carolina (1689-1729) and the Governor appointed a Council. This Council of State exists today in every state, and consists of the executive governor's cabinet. The Governor and Council were the legislature and the court.

In 1700 the British Board of Trade became alarmed about its loss of wealth from the colonies. The Privy Council and the British Board of Trade ruled the colonies by giving advice to the King. Just like the stockholders of the non-federal Federal Reserve advise our President today.

The British Board of Trade was composed of the King's agents, the Privy Council and the Archbishop of Canterbury representing the Church of England.

They refused to allow Jewish money lenders on their Board, so the Jewish money lenders rule in America *now,* through the Federal Reserve Bank.

Under the 1697 Navigation Act, the British Board of Trade, established vice-admiralty courts in all the colonies, giving these courts jurisdiction over Trade, ordinary *maritime* cases, and maritime cases of *prize.* The Board of Trade even granted jurisdiction over timber, by the Act of 1722. These admiralty courts, under the Townsend Acts, consolidated British control in America.

"The grand purpose of the Constitution was to unify the several [separate] states in their national, international and interstate relations; all other purposes were subordinate and ancillary to this. The Governor was commissioned as Vice-Admiral, a most zealous supporter of the English Admiralty ever claimed." *(Benedict on Admiralty, 1850).*

This type of court exists today and is the reason why you cannot bring a pure Article-of-the-Bill-of-Rights argument in any merchant contract court of their *private* civil law.

"The civil law was the law of admiralty and proceedings in admiralty resemble civil law practice." *(Ibid, § 5).*

Revenue comes under Commerce and the jurisdiction of admiralty/maritime courts. Every judge states that you can't bring the Constitution into his court. You can't bring the 7th Article of the Bill of Rights into the courts. Why?

"The 7th Article of the Bill of Rights is restricted to suits at common law not suits of equity nor admiralty-maritime jurisdiction." *(Benedict on The American Admiralty its Jurisdiction and Practice, chapter 13).*

All state or federal maritime revenue cases deal with *contracts,* instead of the laws and the Constitution of the United States. Since all revenue cases deal only with *contracts,* — where is the state's contract with you? There isn't any. Unless, that is, you confirm their *presumption* that the state *does* have a contract with you.

The following quote proves this point:

"A case in admiralty does not arise under the Constitution or Laws of the United States." — *American Ins. Co. v. Canter, 1 Pet. 511, 545 (1828).*

"The question before the court is not whether the court has jurisdiction over you, but *what are the rights of the parties to the suit.* It is not a question in abatement, but of the *merits* of the action. Where the cause is a maritime cause subject to admiralty cognizance jurisdiction is over the *person* as well as the ship." *(Statement of the judge in 12 Wheat 460: 7 Howard 729 Boyd's proceeding).*

"The vessels also that are given thee for the service of the house of thy God, those deliver thou before the God of Jerusalem. And whatsoever more shall be needful for the house of thy God, which thou shalt have occasion to bestow, bestow it out of the king's treasure house." *(Ezra 7:19, 20).*

In the courts today the argument should be they went outside of their constitutional limitations to attack you under presumption and fraud, therefore violating individual Articles of the Bill of Rights.

This was an overly simplified statement.

Don't get enticed into claiming that the Bill of Rights amend the Constitution. The Bill of Rights has its *own* Preamble that few people know of today. The Bill of Rights is *separate and distinct* from the Constitution.

The Bill of Rights doesn't amend *anything* in the body of the Constitution. If it did, point to the specific part of the Constitution that the Second Article of the Bill of Rights changed. — You can't.

As a private man, you cannot claim a constitutional breach. *(Padleford Case, 14 Ga. 438).* You can claim a breach of their fiduciary responsibility to you regarding any Article of the Bill of Rights regarding your "God bestowed Rights.

Note well the sequence of events in the actions below.

1712. The Proprietors elect Edward Hyde as an "Independent Governor" to separate North Carolina from South Carolina.

1729. Seven of the Proprietors transfer their shares of stock back to the British Crown. The only holdout is Sir George Carteret. He retains 1/8th of the original 1665 Grant until he looses it in the Revolutionary War.

1751, March. The Restraining Act, presented to Parliament by the British Board of Trade, bars the Colonies from issuing paper money and letters of credit. This gives the King's orders the validity of formal law in America, but the Colonies don't honor the restraint because it destroys colonial control over colonial trade.

No gold or silver was being mined in America at that time. They had to buy gold and silver from other countries. And England had the most gold.

1754, July. The Confederacy is established so that the colonists can issue paper money on their own. Benjamin Franklin had long before advocated doing this.

1774, August. The American Revolution did not start with "the shot heard 'round the world" (when the British Regulars fired upon a small group of hastily assembled patriots on the Massachusetts Lexington Green on the morning of April 19, 1775).

Starting in August 1774, the plain farmers and craftsmen of Massachusetts, guarding their liberties jealously and voting at every turn, wrested control from the most powerful empire on earth. Gathering under no special leadership, the people of rural Massachusetts, which included Maine at that time, rose up and completely, and forcibly, overthrew the established government, and began to set up a government of their own.

1775, March. The Pennsylvania Assembly borrows money and issues bills of credit without the authorization of the Governor or the King, so the British Board of Trade institutes the gold standard in the Colonies whereby the only money the colonists are authorized to use is silver and gold coin. The effect of this leads to commercial depression and a clamor for independence from the Crown.

Benjamin Franklin says that paper money served as a medium of credit and exchange. That its use made possible the outstanding growth of the Colonies and their trade. The Tories argue that paper money issued by the colonists overrides British control of American wealth.

July 4, 1776. The Declaration of Independence is devised by British agents to *foment* a Revolutionary War that would bankrupt the Colonies and prepare the way for an American Constitution that would override the Articles of Confederation and ban the use of letters of credit and paper money in *covert* support of the British Board of Trade.

This explains why our colonial government denied itself the power to issue currency other that coin, or to charter banks, forcing it to borrow money at interest from a private bank named the Bank of the United States, forerunner of

Let The Truth Be Known   15

the non-federal Federal Reserve at the government's expense.

1777-1782. To finance the Revolutionary War. The colonists were forced to borrow heavily from the King of France, *who was also the King of England they were fighting against.* The colonists end up owing 18 million liras to the King of France, *who is also the king of England,* as the war cost of revolting against the Crown.

1782. This debt is acknowledged by promising a U.S. Constitution as a concession that ends the war.

1783. The Paris Peace Treaty is signed in Paris France establishing a 6-year *mortgage loan* to come due in 1788.

1787. The promised Constitution is established **by treaty with the Crown** to guarantee that the unpaid debt to the Crown would be paid. In this Constitution, the new federalized government guaranteed payment of the debt to the Crown and denied itself the power to issue any currency except silver or gold coin, or to charter banks. They chartered a private bank *in conjunction with their creditors* to issue paper money to be *loaned* to the government *at interest* instead.

The Federal Reserve Bank is the American **twin** of the British Board of Trade. The bankers put the "coin only clause" into the Constitution so they could control the paper "credit-money" we use today.

Paper is NOT money.

2
Emergency War Powers

How could Congress charter private Banks or the non-federal Federal Reserve System when the Constitution says it can't? Congress chartered the First Bank of the United States, *a private Central Bank,* under the loophole they wrote into the U.S. Constitution pertaining to national emergencies and war.

The new federal United States exchanged $2,000,000 for 20% of the capital stock of the *private* First Bank of the United States.

So who controls the States, — the federal United States and the courts? Yes! The British Board of Trade. And who established the British Board of Trade? Right again. The King of Great Britain.

THE NEW STATE REPLACES THE KING

In 1730, the King sent a Royal governor to North Carolina and demanded that he order the North Carolina Assembly to require registration of all holdings of land so that an accurate "rent roll" (tax list) could be sent to the Crown. So now there are *Two Governors* existing for that State.

The Assembly received complaints that tax collectors were demanding 7 or 8 pounds sterling in local currency for every 1 pound sterling taxes owed, to which the tax collectors threatened to add additional charges if they had to seize the taxed property for payment. (Distant rumblings of the present day private IRS based in Alcohol, Tobacco and Firearms, taking orders from the Secretary of the Treasury of Puerto Rico as defined in 27 CFR 250.11).

We are not free and never have been. So much for the U.S. Constitution that was to keep the Government and the private agents and corporations it employs in check.

Let The Truth Be Known

When a County of a State demands a "rent roll" tax (property tax) he is informing you that you don't own your property at all because you have pledged it to the State. If you *did* own your property, the County could not sell it for delinquent "rent roll" payments called property taxes.

If you *really* owned your home and ever lost your job or came upon hard times, you would at least have a roof over your head and not have to come up with extortion money to pay the "taxes." This extortion has gone on since the Declaration of Independence and The Revolutionary War that was supposed to set us free; or so we thought.

Nothing could be further from the truth.

Contrary to what most people in America believe, the Sheriff is *not* (what you have been taught) a protector of man's rights. The Royal Governor appointed an Executive Officer of the County court who *was* also the "Provost Marshall." In 1738 this title was changed to "Sheriff." The Proprietors had to enforce the Acts of the British Parliament, so who better qualified to do this other than the Provost Marshall (Provincial Marshall)?

"Provost" is defined in Webster's Dictionary in many ways, but it generally means "a person appointed to superintend or preside over something." A Provost answers to the Mayor, the President, the King, or etc. The definition doesn't mention him reporting to the people; 'cause he can't.

Although the Sheriff goes through the election process, today, he swears allegiance to the State via the State's Constitution. His allegiance is *not* to the people but to the corporate establishment ruled by the Governor of the Corporate State. So he is still a "Provost Marshall."

To whom did the Sheriff of Nottingham report? From whom did the Sheriff of Nottingham collect revenue? *For* whom did Sheriff of Nottingham collect it? Ah-ha! He was no Robin Hood, was he?

You would report a crime on a military base to the Provost Marshall (its Sheriff).

We are still under the King's War Power Act and are considered to be the "enemy" of the Corporate United States. They just added icing on the Cake by additional War Power Acts in 1812, 1861, and 1933. Since then every State of the corporate United States has re-stated the Emergency War Power Acts as late as the 1990s.

Don't you just love the Constitution that you claim to have loved and supported all of your life?

3
The Provincial Congress

One of the tenets people believe in today was expressed in the first Provincial Congress of North Carolina (July 25, 1774) in Pitt County:

"Since the Constitutional Assembly of this Colony are prevented from exercising their right to provide for the security and liberty of the people, that right reverts to the people from whence all power and legislation flow."

Courts of common law should be established in each State as a *medium* for our liberty. They should be true courts of original jurisdiction. The people (not *"citizens of the State of such and such"*) would speak through these courts since they would not be courts of the corporate State that rule commercial aspects and State citizens.

State courts do not allow common law (natural law) to be exercised in their commercial settings. We're back where we were 200 and more years ago. Jefferson said, **"God forbid we should ever be twenty years without a rebellion."**

People today have been complacent and have let the ruling class run their lives.

The second Provincial Congress (April 4, 1775) resulted in a fight between the Royal-Crown people and the American people which went nowhere.

The third Provincial Congress (August 20, 1775) created its own Declaration of Independence but this declaration was destroyed without leaving any evidence of what it declared.

The fourth Provincial Congress (April 4, 1776) adopted the Halifax Resolves allowing the delegates to the Continental Congress to join with other delegates in declaring independence. Those in power sent the delegates, not "the People" of the States.

A quote from the Minority of the Convention, published in the Pennsylvania packet and Daily Advertiser, Dec. 18 1787, proves this point.

"In this state of affairs the subscribers were elected members of the Pennsylvania convention. A convention called by a legislature in direct violation of their duty composed in part of members compelled to attend to consider a constitution proposed by a convention of the United States *which was not appointed to frame a new government but* whose powers were *to alter and amend the existing articles of confederation.*"

"Therefore the members of the continental convention acted as individuals instead of as deputies from Pennsylvania. The assembly which called the state convention acted as individuals, not as the legislature of Pennsylvania, nor did they, nor the convention chosen on their recommendation, have authority to do anything that could alter or annul the Pennsylvania Constitution (both of which to be done by the new Constitution) nor are their proceedings in our opinion binding on the people."

"The election of members of the convention was held at so early a period, and the want of information so great, that some of us did not even know of it until after it was over. We believe that large numbers of Pennsylvanians have not yet had an opportunity to sufficiently examine the constitution proposed."

The Fifth Provincial Congress of North Carolina (December 18, 1776) approved the first Constitution of North

Carolina which was drawn up using the states of New Jersey, Virginia, Pennsylvania, and Delaware Constitutions as a guide. After the Revolutionary War the new state of North Carolina confiscated Carteret's property (the Granville District) as property owned by an enemy alien.

The few People in power simply declared the Constitution to be in force and never presented it to the people for ratification. The "People" in the Preamble were not common people but the elite, moneyed people having commercial ties as merchants of law with the British Crown, who hated what the King was doing to them here, and to their holdings in Europe.

The Constitution resembled the British government but was different in spirit. Free men who paid taxes (*including blacks*) *could vote for members of the* lower house. But only those who owned 50 or more acres of land could vote for *senators.* In other words, free men who do not pay taxes could not vote. Why not? Simple. In a *corporation* you cannot partake of corporate benefits unless you hold stock in the corporation.

This "stock" would be your "voluntary registration to vote" in a citizenship capacity that pledges your property to the corporation and deprives you of certain of your rights. This is similar on the government scale.

In a regular corporation you can simply turn in your stock or sell it on the open market.

Here is your contract with the corporate State.

Let The Truth Be Known

4
Your Joint Venture

In 1868 the Governor of North Carolina stated in his inaugural address that **"You are an associate member of the State."** To wit:

> "In the midst of these events we are astounded by a proposition originated by North Carolinians and brought before Congress under auspices calculated to alarm us, *that* **North Carolina,** *one the original thirteen states,* **is no longer a State, but a Territory of the United States.** The purpose of this Convention is to frame a new Constitution for the *District* formerly called the State of North Carolina. The new Constitution, when formed, is to be approved *not by the people who are to live under it but by Congress,* to approve, modify, or reject the same with a *test oath* designed with the apparent intent to reverse the principle that the majority of the people ought to rule."

In 1933 all corporations in the state became owned by the State under the Emergency War Power Act making them State corporations. No longer were they sole proprietor "mom and pop" corporations. Under joint-venture principles all people who are "citizens of the State" are United States citizens in contract with the State in its corporate capacity. If and when "citizens of the State" buy private property in the United States ownership reverts back to the State. "Citizens of the State" are only holding State property in a fiduciary capacity because the States are nothing more than Districts of the United States.

Due to the War Powers Act, property "owners" are "agents of the federal government." This allows the Feds to seek out and directly tax its *subjects* (people claiming "citizenship of the State") for they are "Citizens of the United States" by Congress' definition of the word "individuals" per 5 USC 552a(A)2).

The definition of "Joint Venture" in North Carolina Supreme Court case 207 N.C. 831, 178 S.E. 587 says this:

"In order to constitute a joint venture, a joint enterprise or common purpose, there must be an *agreement* (your claim of citizenship and/or registering to vote for the corporate CEO) to enter into a *[joint] undertaking* whereby the parties have a *community of interest* and a common purpose for its performance. (i.e., All "citizens" have a common interest). There is no legal distinction between the phrases 'joint venture' and 'prosecution of a common purpose.' The effect of the formation of a *joint enterprise* is to make all members responsible for the negligence of *any member available who injures a third person,* and to make the *negligence* of any member available a defense by a third person to a recovery by another member." (This sounds like Social Security.)

As history thus far shows, all that changed in the Power Structure in America was that the King lost the War (*or so they would have us believe*) and a new set of power hungry officials took the King's place.

The Founding Fathers and their law-merchant cohorts were given the "short end of the stick" and they weren't going to take it from the King any more! Or so they said...

Untold History Of America

But they had to...or lose everything that they owned...

Which they eventually did anyway!

State Governors, *whether they know it or not,* are Vice Admirals of the Crown!

5
The King's Legislature Still Rules

The first act the first state Governor of North Carolina, Richard Caswell, did was to make an "ad valorem tax" on the land, on the slaves and on the other property in the State. This took the place of the quitrent tax imposed by the British Crown. The quitrent tax did not set a value on the land whereas the new ad valorem tax did.

Hello people. You still have the same conditions that were here before the Revolutionary War. Only the actors have changed. What before was the King is now the Governor.

Did the Revolutionary War or the Declaration of Independence ever free men? Of course not. The Declaration declared the people to be free from the Crown, NOT free from the Crown's agents who took control of America from then on. If you were actually free, you wouldn't have to pay a property tax (a rent-roll tax).

The People just changed Kings.

Black men could vote in seven of the 13 states even before the U.S. Constitution made blacks and whites slaves and property of the plantation (the State) by Article 1, Section 2, Clause 3 of the U.S. Constitution. This article allows Congress to tax people who voluntarily join the State as "citizens/subjects" of the State.

". . . direct taxes shall be apportioned among the several States . . ."

By substituting the term "British Empire" for "American Union" we can see King George III and his ministers, and logically conclude that the people who we currently say

Let The Truth Be Known

today fought for freedom to not be taxed, unknowing taxed the property they thought they owned, immediately after becoming free.

Would you defeat the IRS/Federal Reserve and once again apply the same taxing obligations to yourself again?

Let's get real.

Raleigh became the new capital in 1792, displacing New Bern. The State Constitution (the corporate state charter) provides for a jury trial "in all controversies at Law respecting Property." This law was upheld in *Bayard v. Singleton,* but has anybody ever demanded a jury trial in a property dispute with the bank or the county today?

It's unlikely.

North Carolina rejected the first National Constitution (the U.S. Constitution) because it had no Bill of Rights, but consented to it in 1789, although it still had no Bill of Rights. In 1790 the North Carolina House of Commons refused to take an oath to support the federal Constitution.

In 1804 the Court ruled that the creation of the University of North Carolina was the result of people assembled in a constitutional convention. A convention is *superior* to a legislature.

Soon after, however, the legislature altered the University's Charter to make the Governor the chairman of the board of trustees and empowered him to fill the vacancies on the board. To this day the governor is Chairman of the Board.

Knowing that the Governor is the chairman who asked for a contract-loan, one of the WHEREAS's of a Resolution dated April 14, 1946, states:

> "WHEREAS, the **Governor** and Council of State **of the State of North Carolina** have heretofore, to-wit: on the 19th day of February, 1946, and the 18th day of March, 1946, by proper resolution,

> approved, and authorized and empowered **His Excellency,** R. Gregg Cherry, **Governor of North Carolina**... to join in the execution of these two certain contracts..."

Whoa! Two Governors? ...and one has the title of nobility: His Excellency?

One governor is empowering the other governor? (The governor of the corporate State rules over the governor of the territorial State?)

Why sure. One governor governs the corporate State (*the State of North Carolina that is owned by the territorial State, North Carolina*), and the other governor governs the territorial State (*North Carolina*) — but they are the same man!

Hey, didn't you know that every specific geographical area in America called a particular place, such as a State, has two governments? — three including the government of the United States. Wrong. Every geographical area in America has **four governments!**

Shame on you if you can't figure this out for yourself.*

That is what is expected of people who call themselves "sovereigns" — *to know without being told,* especially if you are a Christian governed by God.

There are hundreds of documents signed by Governor Cherry, besides the above resolution, that state the same thing. Here is another:

> NOW, THEREFORE, on motion of State Auditor George Ross Pou, seconded by insurance commissioner Wm. Hodges, the said proposed contract bearing date of September, 1946, between the State of North Carolina and the University of

Let The Truth Be Known

North Carolina, of the first part, and The University of North Carolina Foundation, Inc., of the second part, and the Wachovia Bank and Trust Company, of the third part, is hereby fully approved by the **<u>Governor</u>** and Council of State **<u>of the State of North Carolina,</u>** and **<u>His Excellency,</u>** R. Gregg Cherry, **<u>Governor of North Carolina,</u>** and honorable Thad Eure, Secretary of the State of North Carolina.

It seems to smack of a conflict of interest until you see that the University is a part of the corporate sole of the State of North Carolina. Doesn't the word "and" separate two different things, such as shoe "and" sock, **<u>Governor of the State of North Carolina</u>** and **<u>governor of North Carolina</u>**? The word **"and"** is a conjunction in the English language.

The phrase **"State of So and So"** (here, of North Carolina) encompasses **two entities;** the **<u>political entity</u>** (the State of North Carolina), and the **<u>geographical entity</u>** (North Carolina). Since the word "of" means "belonging to," the *political* State belongs to the *geographical* state.

To which, if any, do *you* belong? Are you a voter who claims to be a citizen of the State of Maine? Did you vote for the Governor of the State of Maine?— or the Governor of Maine?

Are you a servant of the Lord (belonging to the Lord) owing allegiance only to Him and to no other? Or are you a servant of the State (belonging to the State).

All land is given to us by the Lord, not by men of the State. So what "man" has the right to say that you owe a tax to the corporate State that emanates from and is still controlled by the Crown through treaty?

It's simple, when you read the treaty that declares that

the King still owns all the mineral rights in America. One king (*controlled by the Crown*) owns the mineral rights, and one King (*the Lord of all Creation*) owns the land and the structures thereon.

Which one would win in the courts today if he decided to mine for the gold, silver or copper?

Who *really* owns the land in that circumstance is evident.

*The Four governments:
1. The government of the corporate State.
2. The government of the territorial State.
3. The government of the United States.
4. The government of the Lord.

6
Are You Supreme In The Scheme Of Things?

If Maine is only a geographical place in America in which the State of Maine resides, along with you, who is supreme? Which of the two can be called the sovereign? Is not the State a corporate religion? Is the Lord simply a religion — or the Supreme Being?
<u>There are many religions</u> (501(c)3 corporations) <u>in the State</u>.
To be recognized as a "religion" religions have to register with the "IRS/FED/STATE" team to get a 501(c)3 "mark" status of exemption. This goes against what the "government" is preaching about the "separation of church and State". . . a phrase not found in the U.S. Constitution.
Government spokesmen are hypocritical. To be recognized as a "church" you must be controlled by the very State that boasts that "church and State" must not mix. Who then is the master if the State will not recognize a religion if it is not licensed by the State?
So one religion (the State) controls all the other religions through licensure — the same religion (the Crown) that controlled all religions before the Revolutionary War.

But what if we are under some *other* type of "government"?
The Lord said that he set His Church upon this "Rock," meaning, in one sense, that He set His GOVERNMENT upon the Earth, not upon some *church* or *religion*. There are therefore four governments in a geographical area.
You can now see why the State is telling you that they can't mix the Church (the Government of the Lord) with the State (the government of the State).

Let The Truth Be Known   35

———

How fatuous to believe that we are free people and can worship the Almighty and follow His laws without the Crown interfering — without paying taxes to a rogue IRS that cannot be proven to be created by the legislature and which operates through fear, extortion, threats, killings, jailings, seizures, suicides and the like, to keep everyone in bondage to pay a tribute to the elite internationalists using England as a front, since it too went bankrupt before the United States did in 1861.

So what ARE you in the scheme of things? A slave?

Yes? You're right! Because 99% of all "Christians" don't know that the Fourth Government is "the Lord's."

If you said No, you are living in a delusion.

delusion: A false belief held in spite of invalidating evidence. *(The American Dictionary).*

delusion: The act of deluding; deception; a misleading of the mind. *(Webster's 1828 American Dictionary).*

If you don't have enough evidence to dispel your **delusion,** there is more evidence to come. We are all liable to the **delusions** of "artifice."

artifice: Stratagem; an artful or ingenious device, in a good or bad sense. In a bad sense, it corresponds with 'trick,' or 'fraud.'

7
The Connection

The tribute of the United States/States must be paid to the United Nations' Bank for Reconstruction (the IMF) through the private Federal Reserve banks in America.

Where did this CARTEL originate? From the British Board of Trade or from the Vatican-Rothschild cabal?

By law, the Federal Reserve gets to keep only 6% of the profits; the rest goes to Congress. But, the 94% that goes to Congress goes right back into the Federal Reserve to the CREDIT of the United States to pay off Congress' national debt to the same Federal Reserve.

So who is stealing from whom?

Remember what happened to the University of North Carolina? The people were cheated by the officials of the corporate State, just as the people always are. Look at school bond voting. When the people reject a school bond, it gets passed anyway, despite a large vote against it.

Never trust a man who claims to be a representative of the people.

Just ask this simple question:

"Sir, or Madam, do you have a signed power of attorney to represent me — or do you represent the State?"

Then follow up with: *"If not, then you can't claim that you represent me in anything. If you claim to represent me, and I claim that you breached your agent status to me when you didn't vote the way I wanted, can I sue you in court of law for breach of contract, when you have no paper signed by me granting you power to represent me?"*

Wake Up! You don't want to be a citizen (slave) *anymore*, do you?

What happens if *no one* votes — or if not enough people vote to get a *quorum* to elect a CEO (governor, president) under their bylaws (their constitutions)?

Now look back to the Resolution of the Governor of North Carolina and the Governor of the State of North Carolina. Which governor is yours? The Governor of your State, or the Governor of the State of your State — the State belonging to the State in which you live. Are you sure?

Go back and look at what the First Provincial Congress had to say about a fundamental tenet, and ask, *"Why haven't people taken back their country from the men who run it?"*

What right did a group of men have to make a treaty with a foreign power that lost the war, and declare that YOU must live under that treaty because that treaty is the law of the Land, that you did not consent to?

Could it be that they have a fiduciary capacity to the people that — *despite their PRETENSE that the people are the ultimate sovereigns from whence their power comes* — they have breached by the fraud they have committed upon the people?

Now that you are up to speed as to what happened in North Carolina up to and just after the Revolutionary War, let's look at the questionable section of Article 1 of North Carolina's Constitution. Compare this with YOUR states' constitution.

Oops! I just pulled a fatal error that brought you, presumptively, under "your" state's jurisdiction!

I should have said, compare it to ANY state's constitution. See how easy it is to IMPLY CONSENT that you're UNDER their system? If you remained silent, and let me ramble on, that is your SILENT CONSENT.

It is said that the American Union is perpetual and cannot be dissolved. It is said that the people are the ultimate rulers and when government become destructive of their rights the people can abolish it. Here are the two sections I speak of:

Section 3. Internal government of the State. The people of this state have the inherent, sole, and exclusive right of regulating the internal government and police thereof, and of *altering and abolishing* their Constitution and form of government whenever it may be necessary to their safety and happiness; but every such right shall be exercised in pursuance of law and consistently with the Constitution of the United States.

Section 4. *Secession prohibited.* This State shall ever remain a member of the American Union; the people thereof are part of the American nation; *there is no right on the part of this State to secede;* and all attempts, from whatever source or upon whatever pretext, to dissolve this Union or to sever this Nation, shall be resisted with the whole power of the State.

Could anything be more ludicrous when these two Sections contradict **Section 2.** "Sovereignty of the People. *All political power is vested in and derived from the people...?"*

Ahhh... BUT WHICH PEOPLE? / WHO IS THE STATE? / DID YOU CREATE IT?

Sections 3 and 4 state that if "they" are to abolish or change "their" government. Does "their" mean you, or them? What law? God's law? The statute law of the State? Or the treaty law? Pretty vague, isn't it? Whereas in law nothing is vague. Law has to be precisely spelled out.

Oh, so who is in ultimate control, the people who were never presented with the first Constitution and never drafted it, or a document drafted by the elite-power People who drafted the Constitution in the first place? They not you, dear people, created the State. You, dear people, cannot join the Union, only the created States can.

Note that Section 4 states that the people belong to the American nation, NOT to the American Union.

The State, being a corporation, when joining the larger parent corporation, becomes a political subdivision, and part of the Union. So if the people want to abolish the U.S. Constitution, they can't, *because they are not a part of the corporate structure.* They are not "the State" and can claim no power *to abolish the corporate structure that they did not create in the first place.*

Check all the Original Thirteen State's first Constitutions and you will see that *none of the common people ever drafted, or had any say in creating "the State."*

The statement in Section 4: "...shall be resisted with the whole power of the State" proves that the people had no say in the monarchy that was created in America after the Revolutionary War. So how can the Section 3 people abolish the State if they are the State in Section 4 that forbids secession?

The State is a corporation created in 1776, not by passage of the 14th Amendment in 1868.

Patrick Henry stated in the June 5, 1788 Virginia Debates, that the Constitution squints toward a monarchy.

As stated by many authorities, the U.S. Constitution is a compact which includes as a party the King of England. And Patrick Henry said that he **"was no longer a Virginian, but an American."**

He did not say he was and American citizen, because the compact merged all confederate states into one state and you couldn't tell the difference. In his argument in *The Parson's Cause,* Patrick Henry extended **the compact idea** to include the colony's connection with Great Britain.

James Otis declared that **"Our Constitution is manifestly founded in Compact."**

Jefferson's classic statement in 1789:

> To this **Compact** each State acceded as a State, and is an integral party, its co-States forming as to itself the other party.

In 1831 John C. Calhoun declared that **"the Constitution of the United States is, in fact, a Compact, to which each State is a party.**

Were you mentioned *people*? Obviously not and for good reason.

8
Protection Of The King's Interest In America

United States Constitution **Article VI** protects the debt owed to the creditor King by each debtor colony. It protects the **treaties** that the colonies made with the King and proves the words of James Montgomery, that we are still under the control of the King by treaty.

> **Article VI**, U.S. Constitution.
>
> All debts contracted and engagements entered into, before the adoption of this Constitution, shall be as valid against the United States under this Constitution, as under the Confederation. (i.e., The King's money and debt are hereby protected).
>
> This Constitution, and the laws of the United States which shall be made in pursuance thereof, and all treaties made (i.e., the treaties of 1606 and 1782 made with the King), or which shall be made (i.e., Jay's treaty of 1792 made with the King), under the authority of the United States, shall be the supreme law of the land (i.e., despite anything to the contrary, Treaties are part of the Constitution and reign supreme over all you people despite the fact that you have nothing to do with it. You said it's YOUR constitution, so live with it an don't complain); and the judges in every State shall be bound thereby, any thing in the constitution or laws of any State to the contrary notwithstanding.

To prove these **treaties** are the "Law of the Land", here is what the *Hamilton v. Eaton* case, 1 N.C. 641 (1796), and 2. Mart., 1. U.S. Circuit Court. (June Term, 1796) had to say:

Headnote 5. Besides, the treaty of 1783 was declared by an act of the Assembly of this State passed in 1787, to be law in this State, and this State by adopting the Constitution of the United States in 1789, declared the treaty to be the supreme law of the land. The treaty now under consideration was made, on the part of the United States, by a Congress composed of deputies from each state, to whom were delegated by the articles of confederation, expressly, "the sole and exclusive right and power of entering into treaties and alliances"; and being ratified and made by them, it became a complete national act, and the act and law of every state.

If however, a subsequent sanction of this State was at all necessary to make the treaty law here, it has been had and repeated. By a statute passed in 1787, the treaty was declared to be law in this State, and the courts of law and equity were enjoined to govern their decisions accordingly. And in 1789 was adopted here the present Constitution of the United States, which declared that all treaties made, or which should be made under the authority of the United States, should be the supreme law of the land; and that the judges in every state should be bound thereby; anything in the Constitution or laws of any state to the contrary notwithstanding. Surely, then, the treaty is now law in this State, and the confiscation act, so far as the treaty interferes with it, is annulled.

Note what was stated by the same court, that those who join the State are "SUBJECTS" not sovereigns:

By an act of the Legislature of North Carolina, passed in April, 1777, it was, among other things, enacted, "That all persons, being subjects of this State, and now living therein, or who shall hereafter come to live therein, who have traded immediately to Great Britain or Ireland, within ten years last past, in their own right, or acted as factors, storekeepers, or agents here, or in any of the United States of America, for merchants residing in Great Britain or Ireland, shall take an oath of abjuration and allegiance, or depart out of this State."

Well, I told you that the masses just traded kings and are now "citizens" (slaves) of a State, rather than the King of England. The Declaration took you out from under the King, but left the people worse off because they became the CREDIT of the State to pay the King his money that the people were never indebted to in the first place.

Woe is me . . .

9
We Are Still The Enemy

All Judges are bound by the Constitution to take notice of the Treaties the King has with them, and they cannot rule against these treaties or they violate the Oath they made.

We the American people were declared to be the "enemy" (insurgents) of the State by the Treaties of 1783 and 1792, in conjunction with the 1787 Constitution of the United States.

And again "enemies of the State" in 1861 by the passage of 12 Stat 319 which exists today as 50 U.S.C. 212, 213, 215, and Title 28 U.S.C. 2461 to 2465, regarding Seizure and Forfeiture under admiralty principles — and the "enemy" of the Private Federal Reserve System of Banks by 48 Stat 1, in 1833, which now lies in 12 U.S.C. 95.

For proof that these Statutes are in admiralty see *Benedict on Admiralty,* section 9-44, § 122, Criminal Statutes.

The following statutes relate SPECIFICALLY to Admiralty and Maritime Crimes:

It lists numerous Title 18 Sections, among them, §§ 5, 7, 9, 371, 1001, 1025, 2197, 3614, and Title 28 §§ 2461-1465, Penalties and Forfeitures. As an enemy of the State, we are deemed insurgents or rebels.

Bouvier's Law Dictionary defines "insurgent" thusly:

"One who is concerned in an insurrection. He differs from a rebel in that rebel is always understood in a bad sense, as one who unjustly opposes the constituted authorities; insurgent may be one who *justly* opposes the tyranny of constituted authorities. The colonists who opposed the tyranny of the English government were insurgents, not rebels."

Section 3 of the 14th Amendment shows that if a judge rules in favor of the "enemy" (*the American people who have had it with the unconscionable taxation and fraud put upon the insurgents*) then he would have "given aid or comfort to the enemies thereof." He would have violated his oath to uphold the treaty with the King that bound all United States citizens to the debt of the King through Article 1, Section 8, Clause 2. This Clause gives Congress the power, "To borrow money on the credit of the United States."

People who submit themselves to the United States or its political subdivisions called "States of the Union" by registering their property into this *cestui que trust* are defined as "individuals" in 5 U.S.C. 552a(A)2.

Why do you think that the corporate United States has over 60 Trustees in all the States of the Union? Trustees administer to a trust. The people are bound, and have a duty to *pay* for the trust, as they are the Credit of the King/Congress and *cannot question the debt* in section 4 of the 14th Amendment.

Federal Reserve Notes are not money. FRNs are "debt obligations of the United States." Therefore *the credit of the United States* supports Federal Reserve Notes.

The 14th Amendment not only applies to judges but to all Senators, Representatives, electors, members of state assemblies, the executive, and the judiciary.

> No person shall be a [all those just mentioned], who having previously taken an oath ... to support the Constitution of the United States, shall have ... given aid or comfort to the enemies thereof. But

Congress may, by a vote of two-thirds of each House, remove such disability.

No disability was ever removed.

You cannot get any oath swearing office-holder to go against the treaty-bound Compact with the King (the U.S. Constitution) to rule for you (*the enemies thereof*) and against THEIR principals.

Under the Rule of Presumption you unknowingly consented when you joined the State in its joint venture with the United States/The Crown.

The People of the world all chose a different government of Kings. We people of America chose a President and Governor thereby forsaking God's Laws for man's statues. Did we not?

The Rulers had a right and duty to inform you that you were giving up all of your labor and your property to join the State in its joint-venture, thereby renouncing your "sovereignty" and all of your property rights, labor included, to be taxed.

The Rulers had to pay the King, so anybody they could entice into their system became a CREDIT they could draw upon. They led you to believe that the U.S. Constitution was inspired by God-fearing men and that it was YOUR Constitution, whereas, It was no more than a business deal to protect their assets. So much for their duty to inform you.

But please take note: the Constitution OF the United States (i.e., D.C.) is not the Constitution FOR the united States of America — for the united States of the Union.

Are you a "servant of the Lord" (Ephesians 2:19) or a "citizen of the corporate State"? If of the Lord, this is what the Court had to say in *State v. Knight,* 1 N.C. 143 (1788) 2 S.E. 70:

Let The Truth Be Known   49

The states are to be considered with respect to each other as independent sovereignties possessing power completely adequate to their own government in the exercise of which they are limited only by the nature and objects of government by their respective constitutions and by that of the United States.

Crimes and misdemeanors committed within the limits of each are punishable only by the jurisdiction of that state where they arise; for the right of punishing, being founded upon the consent of the citizens, express or implied, cannot be directed against those who never were citizens and who likewise committed the offense beyond the territorial limits of the state claiming jurisdiction.

Our Legislature may define and punish crimes committed within the State, whether by citizens or strangers; because the former are supposed to have <u>consented</u> to all laws made by the Legislature, and the latter, whether their residence be temporary or permanent, do impliedly agree to yield obedience to all such laws as long as they remain in this State."

Please note the word "consent" in the above quote, in fact notice the word "consent" every time the word is used throughout this writing.

So if you are NOT a citizen belonging to the State and you abide by the Laws of the Lord, then the laws of the State cannot apply to you. Based on the statements made by the Court, you *impliedly* abide by the laws of the State ONLY when you are *IN* the corporate State, and the terminology they use is "this State." Come out of her ("this State") and out goes implied consent.

Do you come under the Lord's Church? (i.e., the structure of Truth and Love) Or under the United States' State church?

Do you Consent? Or do you "Refuse for Good Cause shown" your status as "Subject," which goes to the root of THEIR venue and jurisdiction? Do you NOT have complete immunity from the laws, even as do foreign diplomats?

The question is, "Can the corporate State compel you to leave the land that you live upon when it is the Lord's land and the State has no claim to it in the first place?" Secondly, "How can you yield obedience to His Law, give up your allegiance to Him, to a bunch of agents called 'The State of So and So,' who think they are sovereign over you, and own you?"

Answer these questions.

Have you ever seen signs on State property saying "No Trespassing State Property"? If YOU are the State, you have every right to be upon YOUR property — i.e., property that is yours. Correct? You paid for it in your taxes. Correct?

Then why would they, your agents, prosecute you, if you are the principal on your own property? All phones in State offices are considered to belong to the State, so if YOU are the State, why would you be forbidden by your agents to use YOUR phones?

To prove that no one but the Lord has ever owned the land, (the State certainly doesn't) here is what the Court in *Marshall v. Loveless,* 1 N.C. 412 (1891), 2 S.E. 70, had to say:

> The definition given by Blackstone, vol. 2, p.244: I shall cite his authority in his own words:
>
> "Escheat was one of the fruits and consequences of feudal tenure; the word itself is origi-

nally *French* or *Norman,* in which language it signifies *chance* or *accident,* and with us denotes an *obstruction of the course of descent,* and a consequent determination of the tenure by some unforeseen contingency, in which case the estate naturally results back, by a kind of reversion, to the original grantor, or lord of the "fee."

Might it not be said that this country (America) *"escheated" to the British King from the Aborigines* (the North American Indians) *when he drove them off and took and maintained possession of their country?*

At the time of the Revolution and before the Declaration of Independence the collective body of the people had *neither right to nor possession of* the territory of this State; it is true some individuals had a *right to and were in possession of* certain portions of it which they held under grants from the King of Great Britain; but they did not hold nor did any of his subjects hold it under the collective body of the people who had no power to grant any part of it.

After the Declaration of Independence and the establishment of the U.S. Constitution, the people may be said first to have *taken possession of this country,* at least so much of it as was not previously appropriated to individuals.

Then their sovereignty commenced, and with it a right to all the property not previously vested in individual citizens, with all the other rights of sovereignty, and among those the right of escheat, but by conquest, from the King of Great Britain and his subjects; but they acquired nothing by that means from the citizens of the State.

Each individual had a right to retain his private

property independent of the reservation in the declaration of rights; but if there could be any doubt on that, it is clearly explained and obviated by the proviso in that instrument. Therefore, whether the State took by right of conquest, or escheat, all the interest which the U.K. had previous to the Declaration of Independence still remained with them on every principle of law and equity because they are purchasers for a valuable consideration, and being in possession as a *cestui que trust* under the statute for transferring uses into possession; and citizens of this State at the time of making the declaration of rights, their interest is secured to them beyond the reach of any Act of Assembly; neither can it be affected by any principle arising from the doctrine of escheats, supposing, what I do not admit, that the State took by escheat.

Escheat defined in Webster's 1828 American Dictionary:

escheat: n. 2. In the United States, the falling or passing of lands or tenements to the state, through failure of heirs or forfeiture, or in cases where no owner is found.

escheat: v.i. 1. In England, to revert, as land, to the lord of the manor, by means of extinction of the blood of the tenant. 2. In America, to fall or come, as land, to the state, through failure of heirs or owners, or by forfeiture for treason. In the feudal sense, no escheat can exist in the United States; but the work used in statutes confiscating the estates of those who abandoned their country during revolution, and in states giving to the state the lands for which no owner can be found.

The First Judiciary Act of Congress (1789) said that "all

jurisdiction is founded on consent," the "consent of the governed." You voluntarily consented to be taxed when seeking a representative in government and in fulfilling the requirement of Article 1, Section 2, Clause 3.

When reading any of the States election laws they always say, "Any person who has resided in the 'State of so and so' for a period of time is eligible to vote." Note that they always put "in the State of" in front of the *political place*. They never say, for instance, "any person who has resided in 'Maine' for a period of time" because "the State of Maine" is a private corporate entity that is not "Maine."

Just look at the Queen's law book, called *Black's Law Dictionary, 7th*. "Body Politic" on page 1727, does not list the Presidents of the United States of America; it lists the Kings and Queens from 1066 until the present day. All lawyers look up to the Kings and Queens, as their 'BAR' was created as the King's Bench, in 1355.

The Pilgrims came to America to flee the persecution of their religious beliefs. They wanted *no* King. They wanted the Lord, God, as their Ruler. They failed to attain that desire, to pass on to their posterity. Patrick Henry said you *"dance to the tune of the monarchy at best."*

Not so today, because a *fascist* government controls you through *corporations* that it owns. There is not one corporation NOT under the thumb of the "government" today. To see how corporations are controlled, and all employees, see *Case 14 S.E. 2d 689 (1941)*.

You've all heard, from many people in government, that there is not one dimes worth of difference between the Democratic and Republican parties. With that in mind, here is the definition of "fascism" given in Webster's new Collegiate Dictionary:

> **fascism:** 2. A political philosophy, movement, or regime that exalts nation and race and stands for

a centralized autocratic government headed by a dictatorial leader, severe economic and social regimentation, and forcible suppression of opposition.

We are under military force by Executive Order 2039 generated by the President's Emergency War Power Act which is the Monarchy stated by Patrick Henry.

Remember, the first emergency power was used by Washington in 1790, thereby exercising monarchial power whereby the State claims you are its 'subject' and licenses just about everything that you do.

Wherever you go they ask "where are your papers please? your SSN or drivers license." (economic and social regimentation). The State must sanction everything you do (social regimentation); all corporations are controlled under the War Powers Act; Congress put all finances under private banking and then generated the Federal Reserve System, etc.: for economic regimentation.

Censorship is not yet rigid, but everything else is in place. The fundamental principle that underlying positive law (of which constitutional law is a variant) is that right originates from legislative enactments or administrative rules — that man must *justify his actions* to authorities before he acts. Juridically, this is the difference between *freedom* (common law) and *slavery* (positive law).

Either *everyone* possesses a certain right, or *no one* possesses a certain right.

The "corporate fiction of the State" (your strawman) possesses no rights; no authority.

If men have the God given right to travel without the authority of a license, then no one can delegate any authority to the corporate State to make it a crime to "travel" (i.e., "drive," for those of you that don't know the difference in law) without first getting permission from the State through

Let The Truth Be Known

licensure.

    The corporation is acting without authority and is nothing more than a corporate organization of thieves plying the trades of fascism.

10
Commerce Rules Over Freedom

How did all this we are facing today come about if we won the War against England? The answer is simple when you understand the economics of the time. The Founding Fathers (esquires) had money and power. They came to America and amassed a large amount of wealth, as did other law-merchants. George Washington worked for the *Virginia Land Company,* a subsidiary of the *East India Trading Company,* which was controlled by the British Board of Trade. He sold land to *some* States that went all the way to Lake Superior and the Missouri River. Thomas Jefferson had a huge plantation in the South. These men wanted to be *free* of the King — *in this country.*

Any speculator in depreciated public securities would be strongly *for* a system that could offer him the use of the political means to bring back their face value. More than half of the delegates to the constitutional convention of 1787 were either *investors* or *speculators in public funds*. Probably 60% of the values represented by these securities were fictitious, and were so regarded even by their holders.

They *also* had many land holdings and businesses in Europe. Benjamin Franklin even commented about how good it was to *expatriate* every so often and go home to England to tend to one's business there. You have to remember that about 80% percent of the people in America remained loyal to the Crown. Only a small 5% really pushed to gain independence. Well, they won independence from the King until the King wanted back the money he had invested in his British Colonies, now called the confederate states.

Since the British Board of Trade was concerned in 1700 about losing wealth, this was about time for them to *take control of the situation*. After all, *paper money was being printed in just about every confederate state thereby wiping out the Bank of England's control of the wealth of the American Colonies.* The Treaty of 1606 still existed so the King gave those men an ultimatum.

Put yourself in the businessmen's shoes and tell me if you would do anything different that what they did.

America had no Navy to defend its waters. The Colonies depended on trading with the foreign countries of Europe, using British ships of trade. America was not yet self sufficient. Knowing this, the King *likely* said to the men, **"I will seize all your property and businesses in England under escheat. I will run a blockade on the ocean and permit no trading to be carried on with America. I will have total control of the time it takes for your stores to run out, due to a lack of trade."**

The Founding Fathers knew it was just a matter of time for this to happen, *so they agreed to cut a deal*. This deal was a *false flag operation:* to make the confederation appear *frail,* so they could craft a compact. This compact would take in all the states, under which contract *the states would be forbidden to use their own paper money. The corporate States,* which the Founding Fathers did not create, *were forced to pay their debts in silver or gold* per Article 1, Section 10, Clause 1. This restriction did not extend to the people. The people could use anything they wanted to use for money.

Now you can understand more about the British Board of Trade and its control of the whole works. *A la* the non-federal Federal Reserve of *our* day.

When you read James Madison's Federalists Paper No. XLIII, there is a curious and highly significant *omission* in Madison's presentation of the case for paper money. He makes little mention of such paper money *sustaining the prosperity of the Colonies* or the fact that *paper notes issued by the State of Massachusetts Bay,* the only paper money ever issued in the history of our country up to that time and ever since, *were being redeemed at their exact value in purchasing power as when they were issued!*

The Massachusetts currency note was defined in terms of Corn, Beef, Sheepswool and Shoe-leather, *the raw material of the necessities of life,* purchasable for the going sum at the time of issue. This was *non-inflatable* money!

The most sound lesson on money is taught in the Bible story of Pharaoh's steward, Joseph, that *true wealth is not gold or money, but the raw materials of the necessities of life.* King Midus died of starvation for lack of food because everything he touched turned to gold *because he valued gold more than the necessities of life.*

Had the Framers not "cut a deal" with the King in heeding this lesson of the Midus' Touch (and you were taught that they were God fearing men divinely inspired by the Lord) they would have adopted the paper Massachusetts Bay note and we would have been spared *endless misery and looting* by the conspirators.

As Patrick Henry stated, "I'm starting to smell a rat."

Is it any wonder why "the We the People" rushed to seal the Deal between themselves and the King, leaving "us little people" in the dark? Sealing the Deal allowed the British Board of Trade to use its *international banking cartel* to control American trade through the use of the cartel's paper notes instead of those of the Colonists. In exchange, the King would solidify, *by two more treaties under the compact/agreement of this new deal Constitution,* his hold on his property in America; England was very near bankruptcy and had to make the best of its holdings in America.

Being business men, "the We the People" jumped at the offer and a new Constitution to seal the "new Deal" was formed by "the We the People." Was "the We the People" the 80% of the people in America? No! "The We the People" were those few who drafted the Constitution; therefore the need for the capital 'P' in the word 'People.'

English grammar dictates that a capital letter shows a specific *person, place or thing*. And like all the state Constitutions, this Constitution *too* was not presented to the people. After all the smoke cleared away, the people had a *new* King and some *vice-admirals* called Governors of each of the political subdivisions called States. Those 5% in power still rule the 80% of the masses that don't give a hoot, and the 15% who do.

To confirm Patrick Henry's concern that we would have a *despotic government,* which by the way, if you haven't noticed, has been here for a long long time, James Winthrop in his *Agrippa Papers* stated this to the people in December of 1787:

> To prevent any mistakes or misapprehensions of the argument stated in my last paper and to prove that the proposed Constitution is an actual *consolidation of the separate states into one extensive commonwealth,* the reader is desired to observe that in the course of the argument *the new plan* is considered to be an *entire system.* It is not dependent on any other book for an explanation and contains no references to any other book. (meaning the Bible) All the defences of it therefore, so far as they are drawn from the state constitutions or from maxims of the common law, are foreign to the purpose.

This *Agrippa Paper* then blows apart the Constitution in the Jan. 1st, 1788 letter wherein Winthrop states:

> It is shown from the example of the most commercial republic of antiquity, that **such a government can be only supported by power** and that commerce is the true bond of union for a free state.

Winthrop is replete on commerce and that is what a Commonwealth is — a corporate entity democracy. The Jan. 20th, 1788 letter points this out.

The Dec. 31st, 1787 letter says that, "Merchants and traders are our agents in almost all money transactions; they give activity to government and possess a considerable share of influence in it."

The Union is a political corporate entity, a commonwealth, a democracy, no doubt about it. And some patriots say that the Uniform Commercial Code has nothing to do with our arguments? whereas the UCC is universally the law! Everything is done by *letters of* <u>acceptance</u> of offers (orders) or *letters of* <u>demand for payment</u> (invoices).

If and when a transaction proceeds to the courts, the courts only have venue and jurisdiction *when all parties consent to the jurisdiction.* You consented to the jurisdiction by becoming a citizen of "the State of Your State" having corporate business with your State. That is why the judge can sit on the Governor's Bench and make a plea for you, despite your objections to the contrary, because your Strawman is a "subject/slave/citizen/taxpayer" of (belonging to) the State.

The choice of category is yours; but the categories all mean the same thing.

You are controlled by your sovereign ruler, the State.

11
The Masses

The word "masses" suggests an agglomeration of poor and underprivileged people; laboring people, proletarians. But the word *"masses"* means *nothing like that;* it simply means the "majority" of people.

The *mass-Man* is generally one who has neither the intellect to apprehend the principles of what we know of as human life, nor the character to steadily adhere to those principles as laws of conduct. Because such people make up the overwhelming majority of mankind, they are generally called collectively the "masses."

The difference between the masses and the Remnant is invariably quality, not circumstance. The Remnant are those who, by force of intellect, apprehend these principles and, by force of character, at least measurably, cleave to them. The masses are unable to do either.

Nothing has changed. We still have the 80% who care mostly about *entertainment, sports and their worldly possessions,* in exchange for their *freedoms.* Should the government, God forbid, outlaw *entertainment, sports, and worldly possessions* there would be an instant overthrow of the government, overnight.

It seems OK to deny your right to travel without a "permission-slip" called a license; to deny you right to own a gun; to take away your right to privacy; to confiscate your labor, through taxation, without your consent; to continue a "rent-roll" tax made by the King, which was changed to an "ad valorem" tax by the first governor of North Carolina on so-called "private property" not used for anything except on which to live; *to name but a few.*

The other States did the same thing. You are living on property claimed by the King, and must still pay this rent-roll tax like the good feudal tenant that you are. The fact that you ACCEPT the King/governor/assembly-of-cohort's contention that you owe the tax means that you CONSENT to their presumptions of law.

Haven't you been taught to believe in the Constitution Article 1, Section 2, Clause 3? That "direct taxes shall be apportioned among the several States"? Well, if you believe that this Article applies to YOU, you were taught very well by the government-school system, so don't complain about all the laws they foster upon their "citizen/subjects." You consented by not *objecting* to it; it's that simple. And there is a legal and lawful way to object that we can study and learn.

Note the First Provincial Congress's basic tenet:

> "As the Constitutional Assembly of this Colony **is prevented from exercising its right to provide for the security and liberty of the people,** that right reverts to the people as the foundation from whence all power and legislation flow."

Let's get real.

How can you, who never created the first Constitutions, abolish that which you did not create?

The United States has a treaty with a foreign country, via the Constitution, to protect its property. Wouldn't they call out their militia to put down such abolishment or overthrow?

The present day militia who realize that something is wrong, *are entirely wrong themselves.* What do I mean by *"entirely"*? In an interview on TV, a Tennessee militia man said that he and his group's purpose was *"to protect the*

Constitution of the United States." As "good citizens" he said they were fighting a government *"that has gone bad."* What say?

Firstly: They have no concept that *the Constitution does not belong to, nor apply to them.*

Secondly: They have no concept that *a "citizen" is a "joint-venturer" with the government* that they say has gone bad.

Thirdly: They do not *understand true History.*

Is it any wonder that the Attorney General's office sent hither swarms of troopers against some militia groups when the government's own "citizens" rebelled?

These groups profess citizenship and yet talk about THEIR Constitution. What is to be expected when GM's employees (who are state citizens) rebel to correct a Contract they knowingly or unknowingly entered into, simply because they don't like it?

The militia members have to be taught the truth about HOW to object.

If they want to stop claiming "citizenship," they must simply "reserve their rights" and pledge their allegiance to the true Giver of Law, the Lord God.

They won't be banished from this land; under international law no man can be made stateless.

To stand separate from the government, under the government of the Lord, is to live by the "Golden Rule" that He laid down.

Why choose a "Caesar" and become a "citizen of the State" and be controlled by whatever means the State deems proper to protect itself under the "rule of necessity" — *the necessity of the State.*

The corporate State — *the political United States and the district States* — says there is separation to be maintained of the Church (the Lord's government) and the State (the Democracy).

Christians, including the militia, would be on a firm foundation to bring forth the First Article of the Bill of Rights to support their separatist position.

The Bill of Rights is NOT *an Amendment to the Constitution,* since it has a Preamble of its own.

The ultimate law-Giver is not Congress (Caesar) but the Lord (God).

The militia and true patriots who abide by the Law of the Lord cannot be considered to be "anarchists" by any stretch of the imagination.

12
What Will It Take To Become Free?

What happened in 1776? Is there any other way?

Remember, their courts are not designed to give support to insurgents. Their judges violate their oaths when ruling in favor of the enemy, like you and me. The lawyer/prosecutor has a right and duty as a fiduciary to inform you of the entire circumstances involved in your charges; but he must work to destroy the government of the Lord.

This class of men is the only group of people that the Lord wished WOE upon, *besides their associates, the Pharisees and Scribes.* History, as we have been taught, has to be done away with, or rewritten. Does that make us Revisionists? Certainly not, for we are Correctionists of the horrendous fraud place upon us by the State.

Everything that has happened since 1789 is only the icing on the cake for those in power.

Many smoke-screens, dis- and mis- information have been thrown up by those in power to detract true researchers from finding out what really happened to us, *we slaves.* Many patriots of today have used arguments thrown up by the government spin doctors unsuccessfully. And the judges, *rightly so,* roll over laughing with the prosecutors, *all the way to your financial destruction or your imprisonment.*

The bottom line is this. They cannot prove venue or jurisdiction over a Church of the Almighty when you invoke your foreign law in their courts because they *then* have to adhere to the Law of Nations. To get a better understanding of this fact, read the following case of which I give this excerpt:

When a government change is made, from a monarchial to a republican form, the old form is dissolved. Those who lived under the *old* form who did not choose to become members of the *new,* had a right to refuse their allegiance to the new, *and to retire elsewhere.* By being a part of the society subject to the *old* government, they had not entered into any engagement to become subject to any *new* form the majority might think proper to adopt. That the majority shall prevail is a rule posterior (later in time) to the formation of government and results from it (from the formation of government). It is not a rule binding upon mankind in their natural state. There every man is independent of all laws except those prescribed by nature. **He is not bound by any institution formed by his fellowmen without his consent.** — *Cruden v. Neale,* 2 N.C. 338 (1796) 2 S.E. 70.

By this very principle espoused by the court, you cannot be made to "retire elsewhere." If anything, you retire from the corporate STATE to *the "land of the Lord" in the "geographical" place called Maine,* rather than the "State of Maine."

Go back and review the *Hamilton v. Eaton case* (pp.43-44) where they said that you "shall take an oath of abjuration and allegiance, or depart out of the State." Let them keep their corporate State; depart out of it. Isn't that what the Bible tells you to do? ***"Come out of her, my people."*** (Revelation 18:4). What do you need the corporate State for? To be continually robbed by legal but unlawful plunder? Not that they are going to stop trying to plunder you if you do. But maybe the masses will wake up, and want to come out of her too, thereby destroying the State's power over them and you. What is the King to do then?

True slaves do not want to live under the Almighty; they do not want to take responsibility for their actions; they seek many religions to placate their conscience instead. This appears to be the 80% of the population of America, maybe more, which include 99% of the Preachers who preach obedience to the State today; perverting the true meaning of Romans chapter 13.

Perhaps all this is why *all rulings of law prior to the U.S. bankruptcy of the early 1930s* are ignored by the Admiralty courts of today.

13
How Many Really Care?

All jurisdiction is founded on consent. Since the government is operating under contract/compact/treaty/law-merchant-law, *your* law is a **"refusal without dishonor for good cause shown"** anytime they come at you with a demand.

A "refusal for fraud" would be wrong because *there is no law against fraud,* only against defrauding. Therefore, a **"refusal without dishonor for good cause shown"** is most appropriate — provided it is given soon after the defraud is discovered.

Here's what the Supreme Court of Georgia has to say in the *Padleford sales tax* case:

> Supposing this not to be taxes for inspection purposes, has Congress consented to it being laid? It is certain that Congress has not expressly consented. But is express consent necessary? There is nothing in the Constitution which says so. There is nothing in the practice of men or in the Municipal law of men, or in the practice of nations, or the Law of Nations that says so. **Silence gives consent** is the rule of business life. A tender of bills is as good as one of coin, *unless the bills are objected to.* To stand by in silence while another sells [or steals] your property, binds you. [OK, people, how many times has your property, labor included, been stolen and turned over to the tax man, in your silence? Did you file a **"refusal of agreement without dishonor for good cause shown"**? These are mere instances of the use of the maxim

Let The Truth Be Known

in the Municipal Law. In the Law of nations, it is equally potent. **Silent acquiescence regarding the breach of a treaty binds a nation.** *(Vattel, ch. 16, sec.199, book 1. See book 2, sec. 142 et seq. as to 'usucaption' and 'prescription', and sec. 208 as to 'ratification').*

Express consent then not being necessary, is there anything from which consent may be applied? There is — *from length of time.*

Still believe all government is designed to protect the people from government encroachments, especially since you consented to be a "citizen of the State" by having a representative in their corporate structure?

Another tidbit from the Court stated:

> The principle at the bottom of all these propositions is this: The States have no power to defeat all the ends of government. The States, by the exercise of their taxing power, can take from their inhabitants every cent the inhabitants can spare and still live.
>
> Therefore, according to the principle of this decision, the States have no power to lay any tax on their inhabitants; and if they have no power to tax, it follows that they have no power to enable them to keep up their State Governments; and without State Governments, the States have no power to keep themselves alive as States.
>
> The principle comes to this: the States, in making the U.S. Constitution, intended to give up their power of self preservation.

Lastly, the Court at page 491, said this of the People who made the Constitution:

> The People of the States who made the Constitution, considered themselves as the Sovereign, and the Government as their Subject. They were the Principal and it the Agent. That this is true none will dispute.

We all know it is not us people who made the U.S. Constitution but the select few as stated by the Court at page 520, to wit:

> But, indeed, **no private person has a right to complain, by suit in court, on the grounds of a breach of the Constitution.** The Constitution, it is true, is a compact, but he is not a party to it. **Only the States are the parties to it, and the States may complain.** If they complain they are entitled to redress. If not they may waive the right to complain.
>
> Now for a modern day case of *Public Agencies Opposed to Social Security Entrapment v. Heckler,* 613 F. Supp 588, wherein they state in the synopsis: The public agencies and the State then sued the United States and the administrators of the Social Security program, challenging the constitutionality of the amendment. They argued that the amendment constituted a illegal tax upon the States, and that various constitutional rights of the State, the public agencies and their employees were violated by the passage of the 1983 amendment.

I hope you realize that States, the fiction and their employees, have constitutional rights, but you, as the average man on the street, do not. Reread the above two cases after reading this book. Use common sense and you will come to the same conclusion that many other researches have come to. That you are a slave subject to the State if you are a "State citizen."

Lysander Spooner said the U.S. Constitution was a **"Constitution of No Authority.'**

The Federal Reserve System is a function of the private banking cartel that is running the United Nations' Bank for Reconstruction for which you are being used as 'credit' to support others, starting from the present CEO of the United States Inc. (the President), all the way down to the county commissioners of each individual fictional entity called the State.

Government controlled schools cover up the truth by presenting the 'BIG LIE' — by painting the U.S. Constitution as some great wonderful "idol." Don't worship and bet your life and liberty on an "idol" forbidden by the Lord. He in effect said, "Don't come to Me, when you want other Kings, for you are to abide with, and give to Caesar what Caesar demands, *if he's your master instead of Me."*

Caesar is the State your "representatives" represent; they do not represent you.

You give your consent by your silence.

14
Natural Law Is The Way To Go

Nothing is new under the Son. Some people want to live under Natural Law and be self-governed, while the 80% would rather live under the dictates of a King/President/Governor whose statutes defy a logical man's conclusions, regarding their statutes, unless he knows the crafted definitions of words given to them by the lawmakers.

Natural law, when compared with statutory and constitutional law, is the only thing that gives certainty to a large portion of statutory and constitutional law.

The words in which statutes and constitutions are written are susceptible of many different meanings — meanings widely different from, and often directly opposite to each other, in their bearing on man's rights. Judges can make anything they please out of them. Hence the necessity of a rule of interpretation. And this rule of thumb is that *the language of statutes and constitutions shall be construed, as nearly as possible, consistently with natural law.*

Natural law is a thing certain in itself; it is capable of being learned. It assumes that it actually is understood by the legislators and judges who make and interpret the written law. It assumes further that they (the legislators and judges) are incompetent to make and interpret the written law unless they previously understand the natural law applicable to the same subject. It assumes as well that the people must understand the natural law before they can understand the written law. **Though the words contain the law, the words themselves are not the law.** Were the words themselves the law, each single written law would be liable to embrace many different laws, to wit, as many different laws as there are different senses, and different combinations of senses, in which each and all the words are capable of being taken.

Take for example, The Constitution of the United States. By adopting one or another sense of the single word "free", the whole instrument is changed. Yet the word "free" is capable of some ten or twenty different senses. So, by changing the sense of that single word, some ten or twenty different constitutions could be made out of the same written instrument.

But there are, we will suppose, a thousand other words in the Constitution, each of which is capable of from two to ten different senses. So, by changing the sense of a single word at a time, several thousands of constitutions would be made. Therefore, where written laws differ from the natural, they are to be condemned. They are useless repetitions, introducing labor and obscurity, or they may be positive violations of man's rights.

You may have read the story of Hitler. That "I didn't care that they came after the baker because I was not a baker. I didn't care that they came after the teacher because I was not a teacher. I didn't care that they came after the preacher because I was not a preacher, etc., but eventually they came after me..."

The "I" remained silent and consented to his demise under that maxim. Are you any different? Of course not, We all play a part in the fraud without even realizing it. The author was that way until he experienced many decades of his life. But by then, all the rights that he had had, had been gradually dispatched.

You've heard the spin given by the courts, and those in power, that **"We wouldn't have any State government if you didn't pay taxes."** The video, *Braveheart,* shows how Kings rule other people, even kings-to-be. It is more than a movie; it shows the ends men will go to, to obtain power, and their deceit in doing so, — and that is just what happened with the Founding Fathers. They were no different in destroying our rights **"for the good of the corporate fiction."** This is the Rule of Necessity stated by the Court in *Cohens v. Virginia* in 1821 that assured that the State will not fall. This is due to the Court's decision in *Martin v. Hunter's Lessee,* in 1816, that federal United States courts have the right to review any State court's decision. Why? Because the States gave up their sovereignty — *contrary to what we have been taught.*

Go back and read the *Padleford sales tax* case (see p.71).

The principle comes down to this: **In making the U.S. Constitution the States gave up their power of self-preservation.**

15
Your Consent

When it comes to consent, the words of Lysander Spooner in the 'Appendix' of his *Essays of Trial by Jury* - entitled 'Taxation' - are most relevant.

> It is a principle of Common Law, as it is a law of nature and of common sense, that no man can be taxed without his personal consent. The Common Law knew nothing of the system which now prevails in England, of "presuming" a man's consent to be taxed because some pretended representative (Strawman), whom he never authorized to act for him, has taken it upon "himself" to consent that the man may be taxed. This is one of the many frauds on the Common Law and the English Constitution which have been introduced since the Magna Carta. Having finally established itself in England, it has been stupidly and servilely repeated and submitted to in the United States.
>
> If trial by jury were reestablished, the Common Law principle of taxation would be re-established *with* it; for it is not to be supposed that juries would enforce a tax upon an individual which he had never agreed to pay.
>
> "Taxation without consent" is plain robbery when enforced against one man, or when enforced against millions; and it is not to be imagined that juries would be blind to so self-evident a principle.
>
> [Sorry Lysander, people are unaware today and have no idea what natural (common) Law is all

about and consistently rule for the State, when the judge orders them to.]

Taking a man's money without his consent, is as much robbery, when it is done by millions of men acting in concert and calling themselves Government, as when it is done by a single individual acting on his own responsibility and calling himself a Highwayman. Neither the numbers engaged in the act, nor the different characters they assume as a cover for the act, alter the nature of the act itself.

If the government can take a man's money without his consent, there is no limit to the additional tyranny it may practice against him; for with his money the government can hire soldiers to stand over him, keep him in subjection, plunder him at their discretion, and kill him if he resists. Governments will always do this as they everywhere and always have done, except where the 'Common Law' principle has been established. [evidence *Kahl, Scott, Weaver, and Waco,* to name a few instances]

It is the first principle, therefore, the very *sine gua non* of political freedom, that a man can be taxed only by his 'personal' consent. And the establishment of this principle, with trial by jury, insures "freedom of course" because:

1. No man would pay his money unless he had first contracted for such a government as he was willing to support. (your contract plain and simple, is that you declared yourself to be a "citizen of the State").

2. Unless the government then kept itself within the terms of its Contract, juries would not enforce the payment of the tax.

Besides, the agreement to be taxed would probably be entered into for but one year at a time. If in that year, the government proved itself inefficient or tyrannical, to any serious degree, the contract would not be renewed.

The dissatisfied parties, if sufficiently numerous for a new organization, would form themselves into a *separate association* for mutual protection. If not sufficiently numerous for that purpose, those who were conscientious would *forgo all governmental protection,* rather than contribute to the support of a government which they deemed to be unjust.

List all the protections your government gives you, when the Supreme Court of the United State declared that the police are not formed to protect lives, only property. Has your government protected you from *robbery, rape, carjacking, etc., etc.?* These crimes still go on, don't they?

All legitimate government is a "mutual insurance company" voluntarily agreed upon by the parties to it for the protection of their rights against wrongdoers. In its so-called voluntary character it is similar to an "association for mutual protection" against fire or shipwreck.

The political insurance company, or government, has no more right, in nature or reason, to assume a man's consent to be protected by it, and to be taxed for that protection, when he has given no actual consent, than a fire or marine insurance company has to assume a man's consent to be protected by it, and to pay the premium, when his actual consent has never been given.

To take a man's property without his consent is robbery; and to *assume* his consent where no actual consent is given, makes the taking *non the less* robbery. If it did, the highwayman has the same right to assume a man's consent to part with his purse, than any other man or body of men can have. His assumption would afford as much moral justification for his robbery as does a like assumption on the part of the government for taking a man's property without his consent.

The government's pretense of protecting him as an equivalent for the taxation, affords no justification. It is for himself to decide whether he desires such protection, as the government has no more right than any other insurance company to **impose** it upon him or make him pay for it.

impose: (as found in title 26, "the tax is hereby imposed") means *"dictated, forced upon, inflicted."* This doesn't sound like *voluntary,* does, it?

Trial by one's peers, and no taxation without consent, were the two pillars of English liberty (when England had any liberty) and the first principles of the Common Law. They mutually sustain each other and neither can stand without the other. Without both, no people have any guarantee of their freedom. With both, no people can be enslaved.

In Lysander's footnote, it is proven that the "alphabet agencies" of the States and the United States, and their officers erroneously called police, have total control over all the people. The courts, as you well know, are not for the justice of men. They are for the justice of those in control, because everything we do is against the system of the authorities who continue to run the system.

Here is Lysander's footnote:

> Trial by the one's peers, and no taxation without consent, mutually sustain each other, and can be sustained only by each other, for the following two reasons:
>
> 1. Juries would refuse to enforce a tax against a man who had never agreed to pay it. They would also protect men in forcibly resisting the collection of taxes to which they had never consented. Otherwise the jurors would authorize the government to tax *themselves* without their consent — a thing which no sane jurist would be likely to do.

This does not apply in today's world because the people on the juries obey whatever the judge tells them to do. Every juror today believes that if you get away with not paying taxes, the government would disintegrate and the authorities would not be able to wallow in the hog trough and receive all the benefits to which they are supposedly "entitled." Never will they allow people like you and me on a jury; and if they did we would be held in contempt of court if going against what the judge says, because juries are now only "advisory committees" for the maritime courts. This is why you will *never* get a fully informed jury under their system. Back to the quote.

> 2. On the other hand, the principle of no taxation without consent would sustain trial by one's peers, because men in general would not consent to be taxed for the support of a government under which trial by one's peers was not secured. Thus these two principles mutually sustain each other.

In these two ways, then, trial by the country would sustain the principle of no taxation without consent. But, if either one of these principles were broken down the other would fall with it, and for these reasons [here Spooner is right, in where we are today]:

> 1. If trial by one's peers were broken down, the principle of no taxation without consent would fall with it, because the government would then be able to tax the people without their consent, inasmuch as the legal tribunals would be mere tools of the government, and would enforce such taxation, and punish men for resisting such taxation, as the government ordered.
> 2. On the other hand, if the principle of no taxation without consent were broken down, trial by one's peers would fall with it, because the government, if it could tax people without their consent, would of course, take enough of their money to enable it to employ all the force necessary for sustaining its own tribunals (in the place of juries) executing their decrees.

Have you had enough force applied yet to make you sit up? Courts of Common Law that people are attempting to set up are a natural law right.

This is the other insurance that Spooner was talking about that can be set up. Those of you who want to live under oppression, fine; we will not dictate what you should want. But don't you dictate to us.

To show either the correctness or total lack of knowledge of the term "common law" by a federal judge, I quote from *B & W Taxi Co. v. B & Y Taxi Co. 276 US 518,* where the judge is telling you that the common law is a fallacy:

> Books written about any branch of the common law treat it as a unit, cite cases from this Court, from the Circuit court of Appeals, from the State

Courts, from England indiscriminately, and criticize them as right or wrong according to the writer's notion of a single theory.

If there were such a transcendental body of law outside of any particular State, but obligatory within it unless and until changed by statute, the Courts of the United States might be right in using their independent judgement as to what it was. But there is no such body of law.

Law is a word used with different meanings, but law in the sense in which courts speak of today does not exist without some definite authority behind it.

Oh, so the Lord *does* have definite authority for His Common (neutral) law written in the Bible.

This is evidenced by Congress declaring by *Public Law 97-280, 96 Stat 1211,* that **"The formative influence of the Bible has been good for our Nation. Our national need is to study and apply the teachings of the Holy Scriptures."**

So don't let the officials tell you that there is no longer a common law. Hit them back by saying that it is true that the English common law has been done away with, but the Lord's common law still exists. The English Common law is the law of this land, because the Supreme Court uses it exclusively. They have to, under the King's dictate under the Treaties.

Read the *American Bar Journal, No. 6,* June 1938 (unbound Vol. XXIV), an article entitled *What Has Happened to Federal Jurisprudence?* by Albert J. Schweppe.

The English Common law that is used was bastardized by the King *after* 1066 and became *Patriarchal law* (public policy) when William the Conqueror took control. This is what we have today. The common law that we want is

God's Natural Common law.

Under the English Common law (after being conquered by William the Conqueror) the English people no longer owned their land by allodial title; they lost the use of the forests when William took them as preserves. Sounds just like today in America, wouldn't you say?

And this is the law you common law people want?

The Magna Carta was not the beginning of the Common Law. It existed all the way back in *Genesis,* long before Moses came into being. What did Spooner say in the beginning of this Chapter about common law?

Sorry, but you are dealing with incompetent cheats, except when it comes to their written law of public policy that assures their livelihood at your expense.

The following is a statement by a Supreme Court judge in his dissenting opinion that shows the incompetence, even of patriotic attorneys that do not know they are in admiralty proceedings in revenue collection cases.

> To the extent, that admiralty proceedings differ from the civil procedure, it is a mystery to most trial and appellate judges, and to the non-specialist lawyer who finds himself, sometime to his surprise, involved in a case cognizable only on the admiralty "side" of the court.
>
> "Admiralty practice" is a unique system of substantive laws and procedures with which members of this Court are singularly deficient in experience.
>
> (*Unification Act of 1964, 34 FRD 325, quoting, Black Diamond S.S. Corp. v Stewart & Sons, 336 U.S. 386, 403, 69 S/Ct/ 622, 931. Ed. 754*).

16
Merge With The Modern Times

All revenue is collected under maritime principles. In this country, revenue causes had so long been the subject of Admiralty cognizance that Congress considered them as civil causes of Admiralty/Maritime jurisdiction. This gives exclusive admiralty and maritime jurisdiction to the district courts as courts of the law of nations.

> It is abundantly established that by the grant of admiralty and maritime jurisdiction, the national government took over the traditional body of rules, precepts and practices known to lawyers and legislators as maritime law, so far as the courts invested with admiralty jurisdiction should accept and apply them. — *Benedict on Admiralty, 7th Ed. Jurisdiction, § 104.*
>
> The words of the Constitution must be taken to refer to the admiralty and maritime jurisdiction of England (from whose code and practice we derive our systems of jurisprudence and generally speaking, obtain the best glossary) per Justice Washington. — *U.S. v. M'Gill, 4 U.S. 426, 1 L.Ed. 844.*

The Compact (the Constitution) embraced the Navigation Act (Townsend Act) introduced by the British Board of Trade, where maritime controlled all the courts. All Insurance, and that includes Social Security because they claim it is insurance even though it is not, is subject to this law.

To digress for a moment on Social Security Insurance, we quote from *Analysis of The Social Security System Hearings Before a Subcommittee of the Committee on*

Ways and Means, House of Representatives, Eighty-Third Congress, November 27, 1953, Part 6, starting on page 881:

Mr. Winn. Did the social security law as enacted on August 14, 1935, designate the Title II arrangements as insurance, Mr. Altmeyer?

Mr. Altmeyer. No. It did not.

* * * *

Mr. Altmeyer. In justice to Mr. White, and because of the importance of this legal question, which I have no doubt will be raised, and has been raised by the Chairman of the subcommittee on previous occasions, it is important to note that Mr. White uses this expression "insurance contract" not as a lawyer would use that term. This insurance is established as a matter of statutory right. There is no contract between the beneficiary and the Government.

Mr. Dingle. Congress knew that, did it not?

Mr. Altmeyer. Yes, of course. I'm sure they did.

Chairman Curtis. Mr. Altmeyer, is it your view that Title II does not provide an insurance contract?

Mr. Altmeyer. In the sense of an *individual* contract it does not.

Chairman Curtis. The individual of whom we speak was 21 years of age in 1937 and has been in covered employment since then, since 1937, and who will have to continue to pay these taxes, until he is 65, has no contract? Is that your position?

Mr. Altmeyer. That is right.

Chairman Curtis then gives a lengthy talk and at the end says;

Chairman Curtis. But referring to those statements like **"A social insurance card is an insurance policy"** a "policy" to the minds of most people, in the generally accepted meaning of the term, means a contract that cannot be changed by either party. The people who have been covered under social security do not have a contract that *cannot* be changed by the one party, the Government. Is that not true?

Mr. Altmeyer. Of course. I am amazed, Mr. Chairman, that it took all this time for us to have a meeting of the minds.

Now a Mr. Eberharter makes a statement that proves that social security was strictly meant for government employees only and shows why the term **"covered employment"** as mentioned above by Chairman Curtis, is mentioned in a few of Title 5 & 42 USC codes. Try to get the government to give you the precise definition of **"covered employment."** They won't because to do so truthfully shows it only applies to **"employees of the State."**

Mr. Altmeyer. Now, it is inconceivable to me that the Congress of the United States would ever think of taking action to prejudice their rights that have developed under existing legislation. On the contrary, the Congress of the United States has continually improved, increased their benefit rights.

Mr. Eberharter. An immoral Congress could take away a veteran's pension. An immoral Congress could take away the retirement benefits of the civil service employees, could they not?

Mr. Altmeyer. I think so.

Then a Mr. Winn quotes from a court case concerning Title II to Mr. Altmeyer:

Moreover, the act creates no contractual obligation with respect to the payment of benefits. This court has pointed out the difference between insurance which creates vested rights, AND pensions and other gratuities involving no contractual obligation, in *Lynch v. United States* (202 U.S. 571,556, 557. Is that a correct statement Mr. Altmeyer?

Mr. Altmeyer. Do you mean does that appear in the brief?

Mr. Winn. Yes.

Mr. Altmeyer. Yes, it does.

* * * *

Mr. Winn. I may point out that the Bureau of Internal Revenue had said that benefits payable under Title II, Social Security Act, are not subject to taxation of the recipients. This points out that the Bureau of Internal Revenue considers such payments to be gratuities, and also goes into the question of the fact that the payments are being paid to promote the general welfare of the United States and it has, as a result, held them not to be taxable.

There you have it people, Social Security is a unilateral contract that has no contractual obligations and it can be cancelled anytime at the whim of the Congress. This proves that you are *either part of the United States in joint-venture* OR that you are *a government employee receiving a pension or gift from the State,* erroneously called government. Mr. Kowalick is right on point that *the State's income tax is predicated on Title 4 U.S.C. Sections 110,111, et seq.,* and they consider you to be a State or United States employee.

The Emergency Appropriations Act of 1935, makes you an employee of the "government" eligible to receive these "pension" benefits when obtaining a Social 'Slave' Number. Remember, the Emergency War Power Act made you, the people of this country the "enemy" of the private Federal Reserve banks when the banking cartel wrote the act and presented it for President Roosevelt to sign, March 4, 1933. A private concern wrote that law NOT Congress. Congress had no idea that it was done until March 9, 1933. They were told by "Executive Hitler" (see quote below) that this would be the law, and that they shall agree upon its terms. Thank you Patrick Henry for showing us the monarchy created by the Constitution.

One more point, before ending this short piece on Social Security, the concluding statement at the end of the Social Security Hearing:

> In conclusion, I would say a few words to those who dislike and fear the possible consequences of our Government's entry into the **social-insurance field**. As already indicated, I am one who feels deeply that the level of **social-insurance benefits** must be kept within proper bounds, lest the system get out of hand and become a means of perpetuating a political party in power. Once entrenched, the Executive would use social insurance to enslave the people. **Hitler's control of the German social-insurance system enabled him to force individuals to conform to his program.** Those who deviated stood to lose their benefits. In social-insurance we are therefore dealing with something that could become an instrument of dictatorship.

The author's conclusion, as well as that of many others, is that we are already there. We are social slaves under political dominion of the Executive authority. Without the **"mark of the beast"** (*Revelation 13:17*) (SSN) you can't get a job.

A friend was told by a congressman that the Social 'Slave' Number was his license to work in this country, and he was sorry, but if he didn't get the number he wouldn't be able to work. When he *did* get a job, the Senator's *ADP Corpora-*

Let The Truth Be Known

tion, which writes checks for the corporation my friend worked for, refused to cut him a check because he didn't have a **Social Security Number**, and he was then fired; can't get a driver license; can't open a bank account; can't get a discount card at certain major chain stores; can't go to the doctors without them asking for the **"your mark"**; jack-booted troopers as a matter of policy, ask for your **Social Security Number** as well.

President Hitler, who ever fills that office under the War Powers Act (12 USC 95a&b), exerts "Executive" authority even though Congress gives the illusion that it (Congress) makes all laws and is in control. It is not in control, as long as 12 USC 95(b) still exists. NOW. Is it still you position, *dear reader,* that it is *your* Constitution, and that *you* are in control because you are the sovereign citizen over government and that they must listen to you? Tried it out lately? Humbug.

Now back to the maritime international law.

All commercial entities — *law-merchants under the Uniform Commercial Code* — are subject to this law. All joint-venturers with those above mentioned categories are subject to this law. Since treaties come under international Law and the Law of Nations, all that enter them are definitely bound by the Admiralty courts under Maritime principles.

> In this period, as we have said, the merchant courts and the merchant law are so closely connected with the maritime courts and maritime law that we may regard them as branches of the same law Merchant. — *Courts of Special Jurisdiction, the Court of Admiralty, History of English Law,* Holdsworth, H 71 Cr., L:1.

When it comes to the States, they too are bound by this law when collecting revenue, because the court stated:

> The role of the States in the development of maritime law is a role whose significance is rooted in the Judiciary Act of 1789 and the decisions of this court. — *Romero v. International Terminal Operating Co., 1959, 358 U.S. 354, 70 S.ct. 468, 3 L.Ed. 2d 368.*

And they also quoted another case (Ibid 372m):

> And the State Courts within the limits embraced by this law [Act of 1845] exercise a concurrent jurisdiction in all cases within their respective territories, as broadly and independently as it is exercised by the old thirteen States (whose rivers are tide waters), and where the admiralty jurisdiction has been in full force ever since the adoption of the Constitution. — *The Propeller Genesee Chief et al. v, Firzburg et al., 12 How. 443; also See, e.g. Madruga v. Superior Court of California, 346 U.S. 556, 560-561.*

IRS Agents Are Foreign Agents - From Abroad

Do you know why you let the revenue agents of the Commonwealth of Puerto Rico steal all your property under the direction of the Secretary of Treasury of Puerto Rico? Don't believe me?

Then why does 26 USC 6301, 68A Stat 775, state that the Secretary is to enforce collection of income taxes? The Secretary is defined very clearly in the regulation that is used to enforce the collection. The Code of Federal Regulations along with the OMB and Federal Register state that all regulations shall contain the Title USC section and Statute that it regulates.

The IRS is not an agency that can cite a regulation as can the Agency of Alcohol, Tobacco, and Firearms. 26 USC 6301 is cited by 27 CFR, which is alcohol, tobacco and firearms only. Congress has not cited the IRS to collect for them, as an agency, an income tax, except for federal employees of Title 5 and Title 2 USC 60c-(3) for State employees. Regulations are not needed for Government Employees. Within 27 CFR part 250.11 is the specific definition describing both the agent and the Secretary of Treasury as cited in 26 USC 6301. Here are the exact definitions:

Revenue Agent. Any duly authorized Commonwealth Internal Revenue Agent of the Department of the Treasury of Puerto Rico.

Secretary. The Secretary of Treasury of Puerto Rico.

United States Bureau of Alcohol, Tobacco and Firearms office. The Bureau of Alcohol, Tobacco and firearms office in Puerto Rico operating under the Regional director (Compliance), North Atlantic Region, New York, N.Y. 10048.

Regional Director (Compliance). The principal ATF regional official responsible for administering regulations in this part.

No other agency nor Congress can change the definition given to the Secretary in 26 USC 6301 because it would be an impossibility in law for the Secretary to fit another definition other than the Secretary of the Treasury of Puerto Rico. **Washington D.C. and Puerto Rico are classed as the "United States" for tax purposes.** In other words, Puerto Rico is foreign and abroad from the separate states of the Union.

Since the Elliot-Ness-days, the ATF could not go into the separate states to enforce the ATF laws, so they moved to

Puerto Rico and operated from there. That is why they need your **voluntary consent** to obtain your "voluntary contributions" to the IRS. It also supports the maritime aspect of collecting revenue in admiralty courts.

Do you have a contract whereby you gave your consent to the Secretary of the Treasury of Puerto Rico to collect an income tax from you, one of the little people? No? Why not make a plea of *non est factum* (it is not my deed) if the IRS tries to take you to court?

IRS agents are private and are therefore not employees of the United States. IRS agents are hired by the District Director of the IRS, to give the impression that they are bona fide government agents, but IRS agents are under independent subcontract to the IRS, whereby they work for the IRS, but are not employees of the IRS. The federal government hires IRS agents from the private Federal Reserve Bank. You will never get an IRS agent, in court, on the stand, under oath, to admit that he is a bona fide government employee of the United States.

What's more, the 16th Amendment does not pertain to the people, only to the States. The phrase "among the several States" appears in the Amendment which states:

> The Congress shall have power to lay and collect taxes on incomes, from whatever source derived, without apportionment among the several States, and without regard to any census or enumeration.

"Among the several States" is a phrase used to distinguish between commerce which concerns more than one state and commerce confined within one state and not affecting other states. Commerce in the District of Columbia and the territories of the United States, although within the power of Congress to regulate by virtue of its authority over such areas, is not commerce among the several States.

Let The Truth Be Known

Since the 16th Amendment did not say *among the people of the several States,* you are not subject to the income tax. The States, being the only members of the Union, since you are not members of the Union, are subject to the income tax that derives from alcohol, tobacco and firearm sales, but not you.

Other commercial sales such as gasoline, oil, and the like from which the State derives income are the object of the income tax, not the people. Therefore, there is no need for a census or enumeration, and the tax doesn't have to be apportioned because it is not a direct tax on the people. It is on the State's income and it does not matter from what source it comes.

How else can the head corporate body exist and still pay its debt to the King under treaty? All members of its Compact (Constitution) must pay, just as the separate (several) divisions of General Motors, have to pay GM a portion of their take in commerce. All States that have an income tax have to ask permission from the Secretary of Treasury to begin an income tax.

Any income tax laid on people's labor would constitute **"involuntary servitude and peonage."** Labor is not a commodity in commerce to be taxed. The 16th Amendment only applies to the States. Simple? Right? And you call yourselves **"sovereigns"** from whence all power comes, and are supposed to **know and rule** the government. Humbug, again.

But wait, your freedom from taxation doesn't exist if you **voluntarily** joined the State's system. Remember, **"individual"** is defined in 5 USC 552a(a)(2) to be a **United States citizen.** If you said you were not a U.S. citizen, but an **"individual,"** they gotcha again, didn't they?

A new war was declared when the Treaty with Great Britain was signed (back in 1606, 1782, and 1792). The king wanted his land back and he knew he would be able to regain his property for his heirs with the help of his world financiers.

Six weeks after the capitulation of Yorktown, the House of Commons decided that a resolution should be adopted declaring it to be their opinion "that all further attempts to reduce the American colonies to obedience by force would be ineffectual, and injurious to the true interests of Great Britain"; the silver, the copper, and the gold.

The new war was to be fought without Americans being aware that a war was being waged. It was to be fought by subterfuge, with key people being placed in key positions.

All the Treaty did was remove the United States as a liability and obligation of the king. He no longer had to ship material and money to support his subjects and colonies. At the same time he retained financial subjection through debt owed before and after the Treaty was signed, which is still being created and collected today; millions of dollars a day. And the king's heirs and successors are still reaping the benefit of his original venture. The king is still collecting a tax from those who receive a benefit from him, on property that is purchased with the money the king supplied, at almost the same percentage.

Every time you pay a tax you are transferring your labor to the king. His heirs and successors are still receiving interest from the original American Charters. Everyone is presumed to be a business and involved in commerce and you are being held liable for a tax via a treaty between the U.S. and the U.K. payable to the U.K.

The long and the short of it is that nothing has changed. The IRS 1040 Form is the voluntary payment of a foreign tax to the Crown in England. We have been in financial servitude to the Crown since the Treaty of 1783 in Paris France that ended the Revolutionary War.

Let The Truth Be Known

17
Hello Citizen - Good-By Natural Rights

So how did they, without force, make the Americans obey? Entice them into becoming joint-venturers by becoming State citizens, and therefore, *ipso facto,* United States citizens, but don't give them any more information than they have to, under the rightful-duty relationship to inform them what they were giving up.

The elaborate IMF and all the *gobble-de-gook* of codes was introduced to drag us into a non-winnable battle. It was designed so that they would not have to divulge the **real** facts as to why they are collecting revenue.

The king knew that man has to consent to everything imposed upon him, under natural law, since the Magna Carta was put into effect in his England.

So it is with the IRS. The IRS needs your consent. And you consent when arguing all their statutes and IMF codes. How you consent to their scam is now brought forth in just one aspect, but a major one.

Consider the following two cases:

> There is a tax imposed in 26 USC § 1 on the income of **"every individual."** No provision exists in the tax code exempting from taxation persons who, like Slater, characterize themselves as somehow standing apart from the American polity, and the defendant cites no authority supporting his position. Slater's protestations to the effect that he derives no benefit from the United States government have no bearing on his legal obligation to pay income taxes. **Unless the defendant can establish that he is NOT a citizen of the United States,**

Let The Truth Be Known

the IRS possesses authority to attempt to determine his federal tax liability. — *U.S. v. Slater, 82-2 USTC 9571.*

Notice, the IRS can only attempt to determine a federal tax liability on a U.S. citizen. Therefore, citizenship locks you into their scam.

> Finally, we address Templeton's second argument in which she claims that she is not a "person liable" or a "taxpayer" as those terms are defined by the Internal Revenue Code and the relevant case law, and as a result that the provisions of section 6103 do not apply in her case. We agree with the district court that this claim is patently frivolous as she does NOT dispute that she is a citizen of the United States. Because the Code imposes an income tax on "every individual who is a citizen or resident of the United States" (26 CFR § 1,1-(1)(a) 91985), it would clearly contradict the "plain meaning" of the term "taxpayer" to conclude that Congress did not intend that she be considered a "taxpayer" as the term is used throughout the IRS Code. — *Rachel Templton v. Internal Revenue Service, 86-1363 on appeal from 85 C 457.*

In both cases the people claimed to be citizens "of" (belonging to) the United States, so the tribunals were right in their determination because they fell under 26 § 1 in the USC and CFR. The people consented to the jurisdiction in question. Argue against their codes as mightily as you want, it matters not. They joined the club, didn't they? They consented to have the tax collected by agents from Puerto Rico. Notice that the court cited section 6301, but at that time they knew not what we know today about 6301. But that would not matter, they are still U.S. citizens. Forget about fraud, because if so many claim to be a sovereign citizen — *which is an oxymoron because the phrase means you are a sovereign slave* — how is it that the sovereign knows so little and the government/servants know so much?

Ever hear of a "U.S. Sovereign Citizen" ever winning in court? No.

18
Legal Plunder Is The Law

Government sounds so nice; it protects against all evils; will not let you get robbed by anyone (but them); will prevent you from getting assaulted by anyone (but them); like it **didn't** to those women in Wash. D.C. who were raped — and when they sued the police, the Supreme Court said, sorry, it is not the job of the police to protect you. *(Warren v. District of Columbia, D.C., App., 44 A2d 1).*

This U.S. government is here to protect the states, *not the people,* from foreign takeover. The states joined the Union under the Constitution — *YOU didn't* — so they, **the corporate fiction,** could be protected. So what has the government given you as a benefit that they haven't stolen from some one else that didn't know any better? It is pure unadulterated Plunder.

Bastiat said of this in *The Law,* on defining plunder, legal or otherwise:

> See if the law takes from some persons what belongs to them, and gives it to other persons to whom it does not belong. Note if the law benefits one citizen at the expense of another by doing what the citizen himself cannot do without committing a crime. Then abolish this law without delay, for it is not only an evil in itself, but also it is a fertile source for further evil because it invites reprisals. If such a law — which may be an isolated case — is not abolished immediately, it will spread, multiply, and develop into a system.

How right he was. They have a system that plunders

every day, through all sorts of regulations and agencies under administrative rule that makes an honest man a criminal (not of an inherent nature) *mala in se,* but when some men declare what they decide is wrong, even if it hurts no one, it is *mala prohibita.*

We are going to digress to another book that supports all this old stuff we are bringing up. It is one paragraph from Emanuel Josephson's book, *The Federal Reserve Conspiracy and Rockefeller*:

> The conspirators have made sure that no one, other than themselves, can escape the tax looting at their hands by way of income taxes. They have written into the Internal Revenue Code provisions that make such supposed tax evasion the most heinous of all crimes. Unlike all other crimes of the types in which they and their henchmen engage in, on a wholesale scale, income tax evasion is a "crime" in which one is required to give self-incriminating evidence and is denied the shelter of the Constitution and the Fifth Amendment which they and their henchmen so frequently use themselves; in which their minions of the IRS act as prosecutors, judge and jury, whose every whim is law; in which appeal from bureaucratic decisions of their minions is so costly that their victims have no other recourse, *even when innocent,* than to accept the verdicts that were arbitrarily arrived at by the bureaucrats, *long before trial.* In no instance, except in possibly courts martial, is the Constitution so completely disregarded, as in the "crime" of withholding tax booty from the conspirators and their political henchmen. For this "heinous" crime, they have revived the infamous "debtors prison."

Well people, this is the reason why the United States has the highest prison population in the world, which is very indicative of a fascist government. And almost everyone consented to it. What are the things that lock you into their system? *Simple statements,* that under **the presumption rule you know nothing about,** make you a part of the system by your own consent.

For instance:

- This is my state;
- I have constitutional rights;
- I wrote to my representative;
- I pledge allegiance to the flag;
- I have rights protected by the Constitution;
- Yes, I'm registered to vote;
- Yes, I voted in the last election;
- I pay all legal taxes that I'm required to pay but I'm not subject to the income tax;
- My State constitution forbids you from doing what you're doing to me;
- You can't take my guns away because the Constitution says I have a right to keep them and my Constitution says so;
- I have legal rights.

Listen to the people interviewed on TV for key words. Refer back to the statements on the militia statement back in Chapter 11 (p.64). Make any of these statements, and you have no basis to gripe. In other words, it's like the TV series, "You Asked For It," so you got it. It's hard to complain of fraud when sovereigns are supposed to know more than their "government servants," huh? So please don't use the term "sovereigns" until you know the real truth and the fact that there is only *one* true Sovereign, and you are *His servants* (fellow citizens) as stated in the Bible.

Let The Truth Be Known

"Now therefore ye are no more strangers and foreigners, but fellow-citizens with the saints, and of the household of God." — Ephesians 2:19.

You can now understand that when men didn't like the Law of the Lord they sought a new King so that they might circumvent the Lord's law to do what they were forbidden to do under His Law. Now they are free to make man's law. In America we are forced to live under so many of man's *mala prohibita l*aws that it is impossible to be free.

THE REAL LAW

Don't you just love the fraud that you gave your consent to, to be plundered? Note what was shown on TV awhile back on NBC *Dateline's Report* about jack-booted troopers stealing people blind under drug laws. The very next week the response was the biggest in *Dateline's* history. People called the troopers "criminals worse than the drug dealers" and a lot more things.

We are right back to the highway robbers of old. Police have admitted that they are nothing but highway revenuer's. With all this information, that, *by the way,* can all be documented, when are we Christians going to rally round the Lord and declare that we do not consent to the State's unchallenged tyannical power and control? When are we going to have the courts of common law that is our natural right to have?

If the Constitution were divinely inspired by God fearing men, then why didn't those "Founding Fathers" say, for instance, **"Here is the Bible. It is the Word of the Lord. It gives instructions for all men to live by. This is our Constitution and law of our land in one book, which is law common to everyone.** What's more, it is international law. Why did they not simply ignore the King?"

In the first place, it was too simple.

In the second place, they had to protect their property from being taken by the King. Were they afraid of The Lord? No. They were afraid of their "lord." Man always wants something to make him better and holier than thou, for no man is perfect in man's sight, and he knows it.

19
Meaning Of A Real Christian

Regarding the British Board of Trade — that Jewish money lenders were not allowed on their board — and how these moneylenders got control in America:

Quoting again from *The Federal Reserve Conspiracy and Rockefeller,* by Emanual Josephson, the authority on ancient history and the Federal Reserve in this regard, Josephson describes the control of the international scheme of things and how it began.

QUOTE:

Since commerce and money are so involved in the livelihoods of nations and men, the control of money is the obvious key to the control of nations and the world. Rome's successor, the Holy Roman Empire, dissimulated its interest in money and its power in accord with its professed tenets of theistic Nazarene communalism. Under ecclesiastic Canon Law, even profits in business were decreed to be a cardinal sin, and the capital offense of "usury".

As late as the sixteenth century, one hundred businessmen were burned at the stake, under Church law, in Geneva, Switzerland, as a penalty for making profits in their transactions. Title to all wealth, as well as to the persons and lives of all people are claimed by the Church, on the grounds that ownership is divinely vested in the Pope as the vicar of Jesus Christ on earth. Thus theistic Nazarene communalism — and the "modern" religion of Communism, which is supposedly atheistic — are basically both super-capitalistic, and mask their grab for money and wealth.

Title to all wealth was vested in the Church and its champion "knights" who assumed the so-called role of "protectors", much like present "labor leaders" of today, of their vassals, whom they mercilessly looted and enslaved.

Both Churchmen and lay knights used the despised Jews to conduct their usurious financial operations, to avoid "sinning" and the death penalty that it involved. The Jews proved very useful for this purpose. Their use was justified by their Christian masters as taught by their incontrovertible faith.

Jews were dammed and doomed by their faith and their failure to accept the divinity of Jesus as their Messiah. The perversion of Jesus' teachings by the Jewish merchant, Paul of Tarsus, alias St. Paul, opined the Churchmen that it was "good work," therefore, to **hasten** Jews to damnation. This they did by forcing their Jewish serfs to engage, as their pawns, in the **"sin"** and **"crime"** of **"usury"** by which was meant the charging of interest as well as loan-sharking and engaging in profitable commerce, for their ecclesiastical Christian bosses.

Often the Churchmen barred the Jews, by their orders and laws, from engaging in any other vocation than those to which the **stigma of usury** was attached, especially loan-sharking, as their agents.

This was a particular advantageous setup for the Churchmen. For if the Jew was **merciful,** and failed to extract from the victims everything that they possessed, to "the last drop of blood," he was burned at the stake as a "heretic."

On the other hand, if the Jew **mercilessly** followed the orders of his priestly boss, and was honest with his boss and amassed a fortune for him and for himself, there was nothing to bar his Christian master from exercising his **cupidity** (*inordinate desire for wealth*) and robbing his faithful loan-shark by charging him with the **"sin"** of usury, confiscating the fortune he had made in his master's service, and with great hypocritical show of **"piety,"** burn him at the stake — **"to ensure his salvation."**

The victorious Lombard invaders of the Holy Roman Empire changed the financial situation in much the same way as have the latter day Mafia extortioners and blackmailers. Seizing control of the Church, they gave themselves **"dispensations"** (license) to disregard the Canon Law on usury. They openly engaged in it from the very steps of the Vatican.

Dispensation from the Canon Law on Usury was subsequently granted by the Vatican, in the 15th century, to the German Fuggers, the "Rockefellers" of that time. Their profits from commerce, usury, and the sale of Papal dispensations, as agents of the Vatican, grew rapidly, as did their **"payoff"** to the Church. They were heaped with Papal honors, but their grasping greed and merciless loan-sharking earned for them terror and distrust. When one of their number was elevated to the rank of Cardinal, the Churchmen feared that the Fuggers would reach out and steal the Vatican itself. They then decided that their Jewish pawns were more completely at their mercy, more amenable and safer.

Trusteeship of the fortune of one of the wealthiest Christian Rulers of Europe, whose confidence had been earned by honest and trustworthy dealings during the Napoleonic wars, was the source of the wealth and influence that the Rothschilds acquired in the first decades of the 19th century.

Subsequently, after making a large loan to the hard-pressed Vatican, that no honest Christian would consider making, they became the fiscal agents of the Vatican, received Papal decorations and preferments, and enforced the policies dictated by the Church. It was largely in this sense that they became **"international bankers."** And the policies dictated by them were in effect the policies dictated by the Church. And they enforced those policies through their establishments in many lands.

An amusing story is told of the earliest relations of the Rothschilds with the Vatican. The Vatican found itself short of ready cash after almost half a century of war waged on it, for the Jesuit Order, by one of its un-ordained members, Adam Weishaupt, to avenge the abolition of the Order in 1773, as **"immoral and a menace to the Church and the Faith"** by short lived Pope Clement XIV in his Papal Bull *Dominus ac Redemptor*.

Weishaupt and his fellow Jesuits cut off all income to the Vatican by 1) launching and leading the French Revolution; 2) directing Napoleon's conquest of Catholic Europe; by 3) the revolt against the Church led by such priests as Father Hidalgo in Mexico and Latin America; by 4) eventually having Napoleon imprison Pope Pius VII in jail at Avignon until he agreed, as the price for his release, to reestablish the Jesuit Order.

This Jesuit war on the Vatican was terminated by the Congress of Vienna and by the secret Treaty of Verona in 1822.

The Rothschilds sought to extend their financial and political dominion to the United States, *for themselves primarily,* and to serve their Vatican masters. The Vatican's interest in the U.S. Republic was revealed in the **Treaty of Verona,** in which the Jesuit Order pledged itself, *as the price of its reestablishment,* to destroy **"the works of Satan"** that the Order had accomplished in setting up revolts, representative governments such as republics, and so called **"democracies."**

U.S. Senator Robert Owen pointed out, in the Senate, that the prime target to which the Vatican and the "Holy Alliance" directed the subversive and destructive activities of the Society of Jesus (the Jesuits) was the United States (See Congressional Record April 25, 1916) and the other republics in the Western Hemisphere. This plot, he related, was the target at which the Monroe Doctrine was directed.

The Rothschild-Vatican cabal unsuccessfully attempted to gain control over the power of the purse in the U.S. through the First and Second Banks of the United States. These banks were established under the emergency power granted to the President by the Constitution, as temporary institutions by the Revolutionary and 1812 Wars.
End of quote.

RELIGION TELL THE TRUTH

Christians, by their own definition, claim to follow the Lord. Christians were thrown to the lions because they did not and were not followers of Caesar. Okay, Christians, why do you bow down to the Governors and Presidents, and worship the devised Constitution as if they were your Savior?

"You shall not write your own 'statutes' except in the pattern that is after the heavenly. And those in the land of the place of, and which are made contrary to the WAY by men, you shall not bow down to or appease, and you shall not obey them." — Exodus 20:4.

In verse 13, He commands, in effect, *"You shall not tolerate lies or deception in those who govern."*

Exodus 23:32-33 conflicts with the State laws.

Why — *since the Lord set His government (church) upon this Rock* — have you abandoned it for another government and "religion" when the Lord never created *any* "religion"? Did you think "church" meant "religion"?

Do you follow a religion the Lord did not create?

Preachers are false prophets for they know that no "religion" was ever created, except under the guise of gathering money and exerting power. The "Church" the Lord established was His Government on earth instead.

Why must you have a **501(c)3 tax exemption** from a

private IRS operating under their boss, the private Federal Reserve System, *in this land that belongs to the Lord.* Are you a citizen of the States or of the United States, or both? Or are you a citizen/servant of the Lord?

Citizens owe their allegiance to the State, not to the Lord, therefore, they have but one master (Caesar) that requires them to be licensed as a fiction run by the State. The Lord never required you to have a license.

What happened, Christians? The Lord never required you to have a license, why did you get one? Because the State said you had to? The British Crown controlled *all* religions through the Church of England.

Sorry if the truth hurts, but you can *still* call yourselves Christians if that term means that you are a follower of Christ. The Christ, Truth, will prevail in the end.

20
Foreign Bankers Join Domestic Conspirators

You are controlled by the International Bankers that existed at the time when this country was formed.

The foreign and domestic stockholders of the private non-federal Federal Reserve control all of the wealth that you think you own, but don't. The Federal Reserve System is patterned after the British Board of Trade. The IMF is a subsidiary of the private Federal Reserve cartel. This is confirmed in the appendix of the Federal Reserve Publication of laws affecting its activities. See the Federal Reserve Act as amended through October 1, 1961.

The private Federal Reserve Bank caused the "crash of 29" in order to institute the emergency War Powers of 1917, and revise it into the War Powers Act of 1933 to make the people of this country an enemy of the United States. You were never a free people, regardless of what you were being taught in the government controlled schools in The Big Lie.

Just think, all you veterans of every war, yes, World Wars I and II. You fought to protect the international bankers from losing wealth in those closed door deals with the warring nations, NOT to protect your country. It was all contrived by the money lenders long before the leaders of Japan and Germany even had a hint of war.

The Conspirator's puppet, F.D.R., sought to launch the country into war with Japan to save Rockefeller's *Standard Oil property* in China from Japanese control, as he had pledge to do in the *Stimpson deal,* to induce the conspirators to purchase the presidency for him. Look it up in H.E. Barnes, *The Struggle Against The Historical Blackout,* 6 ed. Stoneybrook, 1948.

Let The Truth Be Known

James Farley reported in his *James Farley Story* that at the behest of the Federal Reserve stockholders, Roosevelt proposed declaring war on Japan at the first meeting of his cabinet, in 1933, eight years before war was declared on Japan in 1941.

During this time, Joseph Grew, Rockefeller agent and member of the conspirator's foreign affairs, the *Council on Foreign Relations,* was appointed Ambassador to Japan, to encourage the Japanese to expand their rearmaments, and exercise his diplomacy to shield the *Rockefeller-Standard oil property* in China. The scrap steel used for Japan's rearmament came from the demolition of the entire Sixth Avenue Elevated Railroad of New York, for example, which was shipped to Japan by Samual Baruch, a conspirator's agent.

Now you know why the first report of Japanese planes coming to Pearl Harbor, Hawaii, was not allowed to get through. It was preplanned to lose the naval base and all those lives, so the people would rally round the President when he said it would be *"a day that would go down in infamy."* If the truth had been known then, Americans would have lynched F.D.R. and his cabinet, Rockefeller, and all their own infamy.

In Europe likewise, the *Rockefeller-Standard Oil* group was confronted with a problem created by the British resentment of the Rockefeller takeover of the Dye Trust, *I.G. Farbenindustrie,* so they could not develop the oil fields in Saudi Arabia. The concession had been granted to them in return for forcing the U.S. to come to the rescue of the allies. The conspirators built up Hitler through their agents and through the *I.G. Farbenindustrie* as a menace to England to force England to remove the barrier to their development of the rich Saudi Oil Fields. What kind of a deal was cut by the internationalist conspirators in the Desert Storm fiasco?

The Viet Nam War was to protect the Rubber Companies' holdings there. You, my dear readers, have been ruled by the money people in power in 1787, to those in power today. Not by your **"elected representatives"** who are also ruled by the power brokers, *and they all know it.* The judges all know it because they and the prosecutors have to stop any insurgents like us from destroying their Empire, and they are not above the law of the land when they do it because they must abide by every Treaty made, to prevent them from **"giving aid and comfort"** to the enemy — giving aid and comfort to YOU AND ME.

Friends, **we are the enemy.** When are we going to wake up to this fact?

People who claim they created the U.S. Constitution and who think the Constitution is their God, have been told so little of the past. Oh, *correction,* they did *not* create the Constitution and have no say in the Treaties made by the for-profit corporation called the United States or its political Districts called States. Agree, and you consent to being governed under their rules. Law doesn't exist in their eyes, only Public Policy.

Public means *government,* not you and me. A public office is a *government office.*

Are you part of the public? — *now that you know?*

Let The Truth Be Known

21
We Cannot Charge Treason

We, the little people, *did not* create the United States Constitution. We did not create the governments under the State Constitutions. We did not create the Treaties before or after the Constitutions were made. All "government officials" and their "employees" are bound to obey their Constitutions by oath, according to Article VI and the 3rd Section of the 14th Amendment.

Did WE take an oath to uphold the Constitution? No. Then are we bound by the Constitution? No. Then, how can we claim that the officials are guilty of treason? They are upholding the Treaties that bound them when they took an Oath to support their Constitutions.

Were not we "little people" considered to be the enemy of the King when he made the Compact and Treaties with the government of the Confederation and afterward the United States, Congress? Were you ever a part of Congress? How are they treasonous and by what act are they such? Wouldn't they be guilty of treason if they gave aid and comfort to the "enemy"? Those "insurrectionist" people who try to oust the officials of the corporation from only simply what their oath binds them to do? Are they treasonous to the natural Law? How can they be treasonous to the natural Law when they are not bound by the Natural Law of the Lord? Haven't they assumed the role of master; in place of the Lord?

If you are a citizen/servant of the State and the United States and take an oath to uphold the Constitutions, how can you cite the board of Directors (*President, Vice President, Secretary of State, Secretary of Treasury, Attorney General*), and all others for treason when controlling you via treaties made before you were born? So what if they gave complete control to the private Federal Reserve to control all of their debts by federal reserve notes, *obligations of the United States,* to use you as Credit to pay back the King what was agreed to by Treaty? Doesn't the 14th Amendment say that you cannot question the debt of Congress? Didn't you know that the debt originated before the 1787 Constitution was created, and continues in perpetuity? Why do you call yourselves sovereign citizens, when there is no such term in recorded history? A Citizen is a servant/serf/slave/taxpayer determined by the time period in which you live. So the term, "sovereign citizen," devised by someone before your time is truly an oxymoron. It is like saying it is black as day; or like a poor rich man; cruel kindness; a sweet and sour deal; a sovereign slave, and so forth. If you don't wake up, and start behaving like the sovereigns you claim to be — or rather servants of the Lord — you are wasting your time.

22
Political or Legal Terminology

When the statutes of man, the law-merchant, are made, there always has to be a "way out" otherwise the law merchants themselves would be bound by their own laws, which for them would be impossible. This would defeat the maxim of law, *impossibillium nella obligato est* — "there is no obligation to do impossible things."

In the tax code the term "resident" is used as a linchpin, as is the term "citizen." We claim that the term "non-resident" is what we should all be using, provided, *however,* that one is not involved with a trade or business with the State or the United States. "Non-resident" is defined by *Black's Law Dictionary* as:

> One who does not reside within the jurisdiction in question; one who is not an inhabitant of "the state of the forum."

Our property is described in 26 USC 7701a 31. This code says that a foreign estate or trust is exempt from income tax. Hopefully the following will show you how the legal terms such as *resident, inhabitant, joint-venture, non-resident, alien, foreign estate,* and *state of the forum,* all tie together.

Just reading the *Penelope case* should be enough for you "sovereigns" to understand. "Resident taxpayer" is a term for living in a political area. "Resident" is the opposite of "non-resident."

"Resident" is legally defined in *United States v. Penelope, 27 Fed. Case No. 16024,* which states:

By admitting that the common acceptance of the word and its legal technical meaning are different, we must presume that Congress meant to adopt the latter. But this highly penal act must have strict construction. The question seems to be whether they inserted "resident" without the legal meaning generally affixed to it. If they have omitted to express their meaning, we cannot supply it.

Have any of the State legislatures or the United States legislature failed to supply the legal meaning for the term "resident" as it applies to their gross income tax statutes? You can admit to being a resident on the street because it is used in the different context of "common acceptance." Never use it in court or conversation with a government official because then they use the legal term. The *Penelope case* stated the legal meaning of the term "resident":

> An inhabitant, or resident, is a person coming into a place with an intention to establish his domicile, or permanent residence: and in consequence, actually resides: under this intention if he takes a house, or lodging, as one fixed and stationary, and opens a store or takes any step preparatory to doing business or in execution of this settled intention.

The other legal definition for **"resident"** can be found in *Jowitt's English Law Dictionary,* 1877 edition, which states:

> **resident:** An *agent, minister, or officer* residing in any distant place with the dignity of an ambassador; *the chief representative of government* at certain princely states; Residents are a *class of public ministers* inferior to ambassadors and en-

voys, but, like them, they are protected under the law of nations.

The term "resident" means doing business "in this State" or in the capacity of an officer of government. A non-resident is not an inhabitant of "the state of the forum." So if you claim that you are a citizen, whether registered to vote or not, and you start a business, you become an inhabitant in "the state of the forum" and subject to the tax.

Oh. Don't forget the term "individual" either. The term "this state" is very specific because the word "this" is one of specifics. The words "these" and "those" are general, and not specific. The word "the" is a specific article describer such as the Car, the Diamond, or the President.

You must consent to registering your business into "this" corporate State. When you do you are "within this State" and no longer "without this State." Now why would the Lord start a business and register it with another government so that it could be thereby controlled? Are you not under the government of the Lord? You say you work for someone else and are not involved in a business? Wrong, *dear reader,* you are in a joint-venture business with the State if claiming any of the items listed back on page 105.

If you can say 1) that *I am a non-citizen,* 2) that *I have no representative in "the state of the forum" that is coming after me;* 3) that *I am not a government employee or official;* 4) that *I have sworn no allegiance to any one but the Lord;* 5) that *I have no business that is in contract with any government defined in the IRS code as "trade or business,"* then your property is a foreign estate.

You don't have to go offshore to set up a foreign trust in America. It is still a foreign trust just as Frank Kowlik proved by the IRS Code 7701(A)(31). One need not go offshore to set up a foreign trust.

You were coerced by fraud (defrauded) to join a system

of perversion created by power people back in 1776. This assured the King that he would get his treaty demands fulfilled by you being the credit of the United States and its political subdivisions called States. Therefore, being a citizen you can't set up a trust with the land or property you pledged as "credit" for the public good.

The reason why the IRS can attack offshore trusts is that those people claim to be United States or State citizens. The IRS looks at them as they did *Cook in Cook v. Tate 25 U.S. 47.* If you don't belong to "the state of the forum" then you are *alien to the whole mess* and are not subject to any of their statutes of *mala prohibita acts* only *mala in se.* This squares with the Lord's Law of natural law. You don't use the term non-resident in the geographical sense, you use it in the contract sense.

Now you can see why the Court ruled against Cook in *Cook v. Taye, 25 U.S. 47.* Cook was a United States citizen who lived in Mexico for five years and had a business there. He claimed he was not required to pay an income tax on his earned income since he did not reside within the United States. 26 USC § 911 did not protect him because he was not "a qualified individual" and DID NOT claim to be a non-resident alien, but instead a United States citizen. Look at § 911 again in its entirely and follow up on the definitions that it refers to in other sections that apply to § 911.

§ 911 does not apply to a non-resident alien, only to U.S. citizens who are "qualified" and are resident aliens working in a foreign country (*States of the Union are foreign under international law, but not countries*) because the earned income does not come from that described in § 864. Simple, when you begin to understand the definitions.

What is also interesting is Section 163(e)(2)(A) of 26 USC which follows § 162, *you know,* the one for Congressmen. This Section talks about the "debt instrument" of a

"United States person" who is a "United States citizen." This refers you to 26 USC § 1275(a)(1). The "debt instrument" is the "debt obligation" of the United States person 26 USC § 7791(a)(30) found in the W-4 Gift Tax scheme at 26 USC § 2511(b)(2), which is intangible property. The non-resident alien is excepted from this Section. YOU HAVE NO CONTRACT [AS A CONGRESSMAN DOES].

How do you get your intangible property back when they took it? Easy. Sue under extortion, fraud and conspiracy (not income tax). Never use an income tax argument, only the fact of extortion and fraud in state court under the *Tucker Act*.

> **fraud:** An intentional perversion of truth for the purpose of inducing another who relies upon it to part with some valuable thing belonging to him. — *Blacks law, 5th ed.*

The United States Supreme Court (a tribunal) stated that, **"We have held that the United States cannot, against the claim of an innocent party, hold his money which has gone into this treasury by means of the fraud of this agent."** — *Stuart v. Chinese Chamber of Commerce of Phoenix 168F2d 712.*

When the government has illegally received money which is the property of an innocent citizen, and when this money has gone into the Treasury of the United States, there arises an implied contract on the part of the Government to make restitution to the rightful owner under the *Tucker Act* and this Court has jurisdiction to entertain this suit. We treat such suits as based upon a breach of contract implied in fact under which the government agrees to refund to non-taxpayer's property of those persons upon which the government improperly has levied. — *Gordon v. United States 649 F2d 837.*

Let The Truth Be Known

And if done right, you use the UCC to get it done properly in their own corporate tribunals, because that's all that is out there, folks, and its all maritime (colorable) international law.

When the government claims immunity under the FRCP 12(b)(6) pleading, "failure to state a claim upon which relief can be granted," its time to ask: "Are they operating under a fiduciary capacity as a trustee of your Cestui Que trust?" This will show fraud if they claim fiduciary capacity.

Let's look at another point that concerns the term "allegiance."

> **allodium:** Land held absolutely in one's own right, and not of any lord or superior; land not subject to feudal duties or burdens. An estate held by absolute ownership, without recognizing any superior to whom any duty is due on account thereof. — *Black Law, 5th Ed.*

Isn't it interesting how feudal and federal relate to each other today? When looking at the case of *Talbot v. Janson, 3 Dall. 133*, the argument is well presented in feudal allegiance and federal (United States) citizenship:

> It is to be remembered that, whether original or in its artificial state, allegiance as well as fealty rests upon land, and are due to persons. Not so with respect to citizenship, which arises from distinction to the feudal system. It is a substitute for allegiance, and corresponds with the new order of things.

If you have any doubts about wanting to be a United States citizen rather than an American Citizen (non-resident alien), see *Elk v. Wilkins, 112 US 94, 109 (1884)*.

Notice that I did not say State citizen.

I have since dropped the term citizen from the phrase American Citizen. I am learning all the time and make mistakes because the fraud is so great. This is in conformity to Patrick Henry when he said, **"I am no longer a Virginian, but an American."** He did not say American citizen.

This Court, being a true Court at that time, removed any doubts when discussing the phrase, "subject to the jurisdiction thereof" (of the United States) in the 14th Amendment.

> The evident meaning of these last words is, not merely subject in some respect or degree to the jurisdiction of the United States, but completely subject to their political jurisdiction, and owing them direct and immediate allegiance. And the words relate to the time of birth in the one case, as they do to the time of naturalization in the other.

The phrase "direct and immediate" are terms right out of the feudal law. Ask yourself, why did our forefathers refuse to make a pledge to anyone but God? Right now you would despise anyone for not saluting the flag, for they would not be "patriotic" in your opinion. So what would you think of the Founding Fathers and of the people of America, if they stood next to you, not saluting the flag? They had their fill of allegiance to the King and broke away from it so you wouldn't have to pledge allegiance to the fiction called The United States that they created. The progression in history went from the serf to the slave to the term citizen, all meaning the same thing: taxpayer.

The State and Federal governments reversed the role and became the master and property owner under color of law of the 14th Amendment, when violating Articles 1, Section 9, Clause 8, and 1:10:1 of the Constitution. The phrase

The United States can be proven to mean only that entity known as The District of Columbia where Congress resides. This contradicts the court.

The 14th Amendment used the term United States, first in the singular sense ("in the United States"), conclusively proven by the fact "jurisdiction" is singular. It should have read "jurisdictions thereof" because places don't possess jurisdiction. The Union representative (Congress) has jurisdiction of the States — not the people — in a very limited capacity, Look at Federalist paper 15, the intent is right there and explained. So the 14th Amendment created a Title of Nobility (citizen) and a restatement of the de facto government.

Doesn't the court always say that taxes are a "political question"? Then you are under the political jurisdiction, are you not? The 14th Amendment reversed the role of people being the master and the State the slave. It was fraud from the beginning, that people who are not citizens are not legally and lawfully bound by statutes of *mala prohibita,* but those who claim to be citizens of the United States are.

Remember, the Founding Fathers had their fill of the King but eventually bowed down to the King when cutting the Deal to create the United States to fulfill the treaties made to protect the King's property, mineral rights to the gold, silver and copper, and his money he spent in originating the Colonies in exchange for the Founding Fathers to control us people.

Is there any mention of the people in these statements? The States are fictional corporations operated by flesh and blood people. Only those people owing allegiance (citizens), and taking an oath to uphold the corporate by-laws, are bound by the Statutes of those corporate States and are called "persons" or "individuals" in legal terms [see Title 5 USC 5521(A)(2)], not general terms.

The term "resident" is seen by definition in two ways, as

either a legal or common term. In legal terms it can only mean a business. In general terms it means where one is at the time that the question, "where do you reside?" is asked. You can't be a resident in the house you live in when you are on the second floor of an IRS building during an audit, when that question is asked, now can you? They are really asking, "where is your business?" The business is always located in the county in the State where the capital is located, and your agent office is where your address is. All businesses are granted their charters from the UCC section of the Secretary of State located in the State capital.

Using Maine as an example, say that you applied for a business license that then issued from the UCC section where businesses are filed, that would be Kennebec County, Augusta. You then operate your business "in the State of Maine." When you don't pay the income tax and you are indicted, the indictment would state that you committed the crime in the County of Kennebec that Augusta is in. The same would have to be for other States because that is legally known as where all business resides.

If you don't have a business license and work for a company as a laborer and you get indicted, the same wording would appear, that in the county of the State capital in which you failed to file a return. This would be absolutely correct if you claim, in your legal terms, to be a State citizen, resident, individual, and so on. Your joint-venture is recorded in the State capital because that is where the incorporation papers of the State and its businesses are filed. If you work for the State you are a corporate employee subject to the tax. If you don't work for the State and claim citizenship status you are in a joint-venture with the State and it is recorded in the county of the State capital, so you also operate out of that county.

Nock and Spooner were right, "The State is the people's

enemy." The State is not there to protect your Unalienable Rights, it is designed to protect the State at all costs. That includes jailing and killing people who are diametrically opposed to the State and want no part of it. It includes confiscating your property and driving you into poverty if you seriously challenge the State corporation.

The State has actually created anarchy. This is proven by the fact that the judges, administrators of the criminals of Congress, can and do change the law, and will not allow it to be used as a defense against their system. I think the term is tyranny. Judicial activism is rampant in this country. Paul Harvey, the well-known radio commentator of years ago, had an excellent article titled *Vermin* that every American should read.

You can look in the Bible and see that the Lord hated, Yes, he can hate, the attorneys and scribes that wrote their statutes, when he wished Woe upon them. Why else would he say vengeance is mine if he wasn't hateful to them? If he wasn't hateful to them there would be no vengeance. Judges/attorneys use a title of nobility forbidden by their own Constitution, when calling themselves esquires and honorable.

Corporate State attorneys draft the laws. The legislature passes them. State administrators put the laws into effect. Judges administer the laws in the courts. And if you don't have an attorney, one will be appointed to re-present you according to the statutes of their color of law. Attorneys are officers of the court who inhabit all branches of government. They create anarchy when they disregard the Constitution they took and oath to uphold regarding "separation of the branches" of government. They say we are anarchists when we don't want to follow their perverted statutes and would rather follow the Law of the Lord. An anarchist follows no law, and so it is with the courts in America today. They follow political public policy which is no law at all.

The whole ball of tar is loaded against you because they are all paid by your enemy, the State, when you try to exercise the Rights given to you by your Lord, the Father of Jesus, the Christ. The authorities claim that God is the ultimate authority in their Preambles, yet rule in anarchy against His citizens when they claim the Rights He has given them, when trusting to abide by His true Law; separation of His government (church) and their State. Need we say more?

The spin doctors really believe everything that they say. And the masses do not want to be politically incorrect for fear that they too will be demonized by the State.

23
Judicial Verbicide

The great moralist, Oliver Wendall Holmes (1841-1935) — a Justice of the Supreme Court of the United States for 30 years from 1902-1932 — wrote:

> "Men cannot satisfactorily relate with each other until they agree on certain ultimate beliefs and trace the secondary questions dependant on those beliefs to their semantic source. The exploitation of the suggestive meaning of a word — apart from the thing it explicitly names or describes — is often the hidden intended purpose of the word's design.
> "Life and language are alike sacred. Both homicide and verbicide — the deceptive treatment of a word with fatal results to its legitimate meaning which is its life — are forbidden by the law.
> "To trifle with the vocabulary that is the vehicle of social intercourse among men is to tamper with the currency of human intelligence. The infection spread to the national conscience by verbal double-meanings results in the disease of political double-dealings in the end. By 'formalizing' informal terminology, we become prey to those who would use our ignorance as a weapon against us.
> "The death (cide) of our nation might be wrought by an enemy whose most lethal weapons are "verbs" and other words whose meanings have become twisted, perverted, and vulgarized. As a people, we would not commit political suicide, but we could become victims of linguistic verbicide — which would be just as fatal to our freedoms."

Almost a century passed before Holmes's term, verbicide, would be widely used again.

On October 22, 1980, Watergate Special Prosecutor Sam J. Ervin, Jr. — N.C. United States Senator for twenty years and an Associate Justice of the N.C. Supreme Court for six years — in laying the foundation for his case against *judicial verbicide,* reminds us that "Whatever government is not a government of laws is a despotism though it be called what it may," and quoting Daniel Webster, "Occupants of public offices love power and are prone to abuse it," and quoting George Washington in his Farewell Address to the nation, "What autocratic rulers have done in the past might be attempted by new rulers in the future unless they are restrained by laws which they alone can neither alter nor annul." (*Exparte Milligan, 4 Wallace 2, 120-121.*)

Senator Ervin's term *judicial verbicide* describes the actions of Supreme Court Justices who "attempt to revise the Constitution while claiming to interpret it."

Senator Ervin quoted Chief Justice John Marshall's declarations that "The principles of the Constitution are designed to be permanent," and, "The words of the Constitution must be understood to mean what they say," and, "The Constitution constitutes an absolute rule for the government of the Supreme Court Justices in their official actions."

"As men whose intentions require no concealment generally employ the words which most directly and aptly express the ideas they intend to convey, the enlightened patriots who framed our Constitution and the people who adapted it, must be understood to have employed words in their natural sense and to have intended what they have said."

Supplementing Marshal's view, Senator Ervin continues:

"Judges who perpetrate verbicide on the Constitution are judicial activists. A judicial activist is a judge who interprets the Constitution to mean what it would have said if he, instead of the Founding Fathers, had written it."

Senator Ervin then quotes Daniel Webster:

"Good intentions will always be pleaded for every assumption of authority. It is hardly too strong to say that the Constitution was made to guard the people against the dangers of good intentions. There are men in all ages who mean to govern well, but they mean to govern. They promise to be good masters, but they mean to be masters."

Senator Ervin continues:

"By committing verbicide on the Constitution, judicial activists concentrate in the federal government powers that the Constitution reserves to the states; diminish the capacity of federal executive officers and the states to bring criminals to justice; rob individuals of personal and property rights; and expand their own powers and those of Congress far beyond their constitutional limits."

"In charging that some Supreme Court Justices are making a solemn mockery of their oaths to support the Constitution, I am not a lone voice crying the constitutional wilderness. I am, in truth, simply one member of a constantly expanding chorus."

"I know of no way we can have equal justice under law except we have some law."

"No nation can enjoy the right to self-rule and the right to freedom from tyranny, under a government of men. The Founding Fathers framed and ratified the Constitution to secure these precious rights to Americans for all time. Judicial verbicide substitutes the personal notions of judges for the precepts of the Constitution. Hence judicial verbicide is calculated to convert the Constitution into a worthless scrap of paper and to replace our government of laws with a judicial oligarchy." (an oligarchy is government by a few for corrupt and selfish purposes.)

"A Justice who twists the words of the Constitution awry under the guise of interpreting it, to substitute his personal notion for a constitutional precept, is contemptuous of intellectual integrity."

The growing body of jurists gravely concerned about judicial verbicide is paralleled in a growing body of men and women who are equally concerned about *verbicidal activity related to the subject of money.*

MONETARY VERBICIDE: ECONOMIC WARFARE ON INDIVIDUAL LIBERTY

Monetary verbicide can be just as fatal as judicial verbicide to personal freedom.

The author has taken great pains to bring certain facts to light. Among these facts are etymological histories of important words related to money, specific examples of correct and incorrect usage of important words and phrases related to money, and illustrative examples of how corrupt individuals take advantage of public confusion about money-related words and phrases.

However serious might be the topic of money in this book, the author has elected to present its contents in the most readable style possible, avoiding a stiff and scholarly approach in favor of a more comfortable and congenial one.

"Wisdom begins by calling things by their right names."
— Chinese Proverb.

This Chinese Proverb explains why this book focuses on *verbicidal attacks* on phrases and money-related phrases and words.

As Americans become more familiar with the right names,

words and phrases to call things, our understanding and wisdom should grow. By acquiring greater wisdom, our thoughts and actions will become more appropriate to our human desires and needs.

As our thoughts and actions become more appropriate, solutions may be found more quickly to the national problems that we face. As those problems are solved, the future for all Americans will become measurably brighter.

Indeed, as we in the United States begin to take *remedial action* against those who have sought to destroy our culture and freedoms, we are likely to trigger the same kind of *remedial action* by freedom-loving people in other lands.

It is our hope that these simple reports will help inspire valiant men and women everywhere to a higher standard of civic awareness, responsibility, and constructive action.

The Lord willing, and we think He is, History will record that this generation of Americans gave their full measure of devotion to the ideals of individual sovereignty in the Mind and Soul of mankind.

24
Lost Logic & Common Sense

Thomas Paine's Pamphlet titled *Common Sense,* drew a distinction between "society" and "government" when he stated that "government, in its best state, is a necessary evil; in its worst state, an intolerable one". Government is "a mode rendered necessary by the inability of moral virtue to govern the world".

The legal profession professors know the truth but do not teach it to the students. They only teach them what they want them to know. Just like the educational system in the elementary schools of indoctrination that keeps students ignorant so they can't ask questions; keep them ignorant so they can't think logically and use common sense.

When a calculator breaks down, they can't add or subtract, let alone multiply or divide. I know of a 17 year old who failed a driver's license test in school because he missed, among other questions, a question that had the word "impaired" in it. He didn't know what the word meant. Many of his classmates cannot read a ruler, even to describe what each of the four lines are in a quarter inch.

That way the judges, who are in the know and have superior knowledge, can put down any of their underlings in procedure. Procedure is all that student attorneys are taught in law school. They know nothing about the law. They cannot, as we who have been in the battle with the courts, bring in anything but the facts. Therefore, all law is a set of facts making law. In other words, no law could be made if no facts are present to cause a law to be made. Therefore, law is or should be called Facts of Law.

The law belongs to a set of facts that created it. Evidence is right in the Bible. The Lord did not create other than nature's law for man. Was there no commandment, that you shall not do murder, before Cain slew Able? How long was it before the Lord created laws for man? The law should be allowed in court but the authorities will not allow the law into the case, "just the fact's ma'am, just the facts", as Sgt. Joe Friday of the Dragnet TV program of years ago would say.

A Case in point from *The Principles of Criminal Pleading,* by Franklin Fiske Heard, Boston, Little, Brown, and Company states:

> It is often said that whenever a case occurs in which all the facts charged against a defendant by the indictment are admitted as proved and yet the defendant be innocent, in every such case the indictment is bad. *p.614.* All indictments must specify the criminal nature and degree of the offense and the particular facts and circumstances which render the defendant guilty of that offense. *p.165.* A variance between the recited and true title of a statute is fatal to the indictment. *p.176.*

So a man can fit all the facts of not filing a return or not having a driver license, and yet be innocent because he is not in "the state of the forum" because the facts say so. He cannot bring in the law created by the facts to prove his innocence. As Heard stated, the law is at variance with the facts and would have to be pled as such. The courts cannot get around the variance.

Who cares, as long as the State can prevail under the Rule of Necessity, or the Rule of Presumption, that you are a citizen/resident who is guilty until you prove your innocence. You can't because they do not allow the law to be presented.

All attorneys get their pound of flesh paid by money,

costs, and fines, and they get their pay from the State. It is well established that an appeal to the State, based on justice, is futile in any circumstance.

Albert J. Nock said,

> This is now so well understood that no one goes to court for justice; he goes for gain or revenge. It is interesting to note that some philosophers of law now say that law has no relation to justice and is not meant to have any such relation. In their view law represents only a progressive registration of the ways in which experience leads us to believe that society can best get along. One might hesitate a long time about accepting their notion of what law is, but one must appreciate their candid affirmation of what it is not.

I see one problem that they all have. They don't understand the nature of the natural (common) law that Lysander Spooner so well described (see chapter 14) (p.75). Therefore they are ignorant of their duties to people, and plow head long to protect the corporate State because they are bound by oath to protect *it*, NOT YOU.

Without the little man to extort money and property from, they would collapse. Remember, we provide the credit of the State. The King would then regain control by treaty on default, under international law, through the International bankers who operate under the United Nations veil.

The United States is so deep in debt by exercising its Special Drawing Rights for FRNs, that if the debt were called, we would then know that we have been slaves to the bankers all along.

Let The Truth Be Known

25
Redress, What Is That?

You say, go to the courts for redress. Didn't the people in the colonies draft the Declaration of Independence when they couldn't get redress from the King in his Courts?

You can't get redress in the State's law-merchant courts regarding any revenue scheme fostered upon the people of America — *such as license schemes, property taxes, income taxes* — to which you gave your consent.

It all started back in 1787.

The masses had a chance to well up in arms against the King's puppets here in America: the Founding Fathers, Governors and power hungry people. Nothing has changed since then. Every citizen/subject/taxpayer/slave is unaware of being unaware that he is a subject/slave of the State. The only thing he knows is that he is a taxpaying citizen.

All other issues — *like the War Power acts of 1861 and 1933, birth certificates, zip codes, social security, that you think are important* — are collateral issues. Not that they are not important, because they are. But none of them matter when discovering how we got to this stage.

When the IRS says you owe them money, people normally go out and research their Code and find some things that the IRS failed to do. They then take this to the court or agency and argue the code, or that the agent didn't give a proper notice, or some such thing, and the court rolls over, amused, and then rules against you.

Here is what happened.

If you are not subject to their laws, why argue the Code? If the agent didn't sign some document, or didn't have the delegated authority to do something, you say they don't have a case against you. You are in effect saying that if the agent did have what you say he didn't have, or if he did do what you say he didn't do, you admit that you would be liable.

This is exactly how the court looks at you; not how you look at it. In other words, you make an affirmative defense, affirming your legal connection to the IRS. It's saying that if it hadn't been for the fact that the agent didn't sign his proper name, that you would be liable. It's a "but for the fact that..." argument. You consented to, and joined their scheme by arguing, when you found a flaw in their procedures. Just like Adam said to the Lord, "'but for the fact' that Eve told me to eat, I would not have eaten" — *admitting* that he did what the Lord forbade.

They are bound by the law-merchant (UCC) rules.

You accept their offer of/demand for guilt, and consent to it when you do not send it back marked "Acceptance refused without dishonor for good cause shown." Then define the good cause/causes by statements of fact — *without arguing the case* (*without joining the case*).

If they didn't properly follow the directions on a form filed against you, the statement of fact would be that *they would perjure themselves if they properly followed the directions on the form because you are not subject to the jurisdiction which you "refused without dishonor for good cause shown" to accept* — then name the causes by statements of fact. Make no *conclusions of law, no traverse into their jurisdiction, but demur* because they have not put all of the facts into evidence.

We just said the same thing twice for good reason, in case you didn't catch it the first time.

Do you think that they would want to bring forth the Treaty with the King and thereby prove that *you are still a feudal serf of the King and the credit for the State?* Do you think they would want to admit that *you are presumed to be a government employee "of" the United States (belonging to the United States) who is presumed to be subject to any income tax, no matter where you live, to pay their debt?*

Now that you have caught up with modern times, don't forget about 1776; don't only think about what is happening now.

Patriot Attorney ex-IRS-agent Larry Becraft has often reported on how *the government controls you by treaties when it can't control you otherwise.* After all, are not treaties the "law of the land"? Does not the Constitution make them so?

Remember, some attorneys have left their profession in disgust, because of the corruption they discovered on their own behalf. The law schools cannot teach their students what you are learning here today. If they did *the only thing they could argue would be treaty law.* Then the citizens/serfs/taxpayers/slaves would know of the fraud being pulled upon him and them.

This information can't be taught in the public schools for the same reason. Perhaps you can now understand why the Founding Fathers were so disgusted with the masses — who didn't give a hoot — that they decided not to govern/control them. Why should they sacrifice their wealth for a people who would not support them.

If someone had to control the masses, why not let it be the power People, and have them (the masses) pay back the never-ending debt?

The situation just mushroomed to where it is today.

People are none the wiser today. The elite consider you and me to be human resources — that are expendable.

A democracy is a public corporation, and a citizen is a stockholder/associate/corporate member who must abide by statutory law denoted as public policy (not natural law) in any of their corporate courts.

People who think that the Constitution is so wonderful, *that they would defend it with their very lives,* are unaware and ignored when they claim that their rights are being violated by the State. If you claim that you are a citizen of the State, you are an associate member/employee of the State.

Your name appears in all CAPITAL letters because you are a PUBLIC entity, a corporate person/individual/strawman named in their statutory law, because you gave up your natural "Christian name" to become "naturally dead" in the law. You are a "natural man" who took-on and accepted the legal definition of the artificial "person/individual/taxpayer/strawman" when you joined the corporate State.

> For as the United States guarantees to each State a republican form of government, Congress must necessarily decide what government is established in the State, before it can determine if it is republican or not. — *Texas v. White 74 US 7 Wall, lawyers Ed.*

So only Congress can decide if we have a democratic form of government based on what they say is a democratic form. Under this premise, we are not in a free country, when we have a group of self appointed people — that "band of robbers and murderers" that Lysander Spooner talked about — telling us that they have the sole power to determine whether or not the people have the form of government they want.

If you were the Congress, wouldn't you use the "corporate entity" definition that fits the public policy of the "masses" — rather than the sovereignty of the separate private man — to further the political organization of the merchant-State? Sure you would. This means that the courts are not government courts for the people; they are private law merchant courts for the merchants; that operate in Public Policy.

Is it any wonder that the courts state that they will not adjudicate a "political question"? They don't want to expose the fraud!

When you enter the private courts they only have one thought in mind, to pay the interest on the "public debt" of the bankruptcy of the corporate United States.

What if the people in the States said that they didn't want a "democratic form of government" but a free sovereign natural law republican form of government"? You know, like the Declaration of Independence declares, where all men are self governed?

Many States have wanted to get out of the Union. Wouldn't this be the logical way to get out?

The United States won't guarantee a natural law government, so doesn't this break the option quasi-contract (constitution) which states that the FEDs are to guarantee a "republican" form of government? If they don't meet the guarantee it voids the compact.

Then we wouldn't be under the treaty between the Crown and the United States. Nary a shot would have to be fired thereby eliminating another violent bloody revolution to gain back the freedoms that we have lost.

The statute writers are clever. You know them as ATTORNeys. ATTORN means to twist and turn around the truth.

Everything we do as a citizen of the corporate UNITED

STATES is "within this State," not "without this State." That is why the statutes refer to "the laws of this State." The action committed "within this State" signifies that it is the corporate State under statutory law and not a social state under common law.

Now you are presumed to be a public employee, so their private corporate court judges can make a plea for you against your most forceful argument, because you are under their trust. That is why the corporation known as the UNITED STATES has about 60 United States Trustees located in every State of the Union District of Columbia United States.

Don't forget the inaugural speech of the governor of the State of North Carolina and what he said (p.25) that "North Carolina ...is no longer a state, but a Territory of the United States." "...the States are nothing more than Districts of the United States."

This fact applies to all of the States of the United States.

26
What Other Authors Say

Another author, Gustavus Myers, whose works can never be impeached, made these statements in his book, *History of the Great American Fortunes* (1906).

> While the worker was unorganized, unconscious of what his interest demanded, deluded by slogans and rallying cries which meant really nothing to him, the propertied class was alert in its own interests. It proceeded to entrench itself in political as well as financial power. The Constitution of the United States was so drafted as to take as much direct power from the people as the landed and trading interests dared to take at that time.
>
> To a large extent the United States, since then, has not lived under legislature-made law, but under a purely separate and extraneous form of law which has superseded the legislature-made product, namely, court law. By one means or another the traders and landholders forced the various legislatures into doing what they wanted them to do.
>
> De Beaumont and De Tocqueville passingly observed that although the magistrates in the United States were plebeian, they followed the old English system; in other words, they enforced laws which were made for and by the American Aristocracy, the trading classes.
>
> From the very beginning of the government, the land laws were arranged to discriminate against the poor settler. [as said before, all governors immediately instituted ad valorem land taxes after

their first commercial charters, Constitutions, were instituted].

In order to accomplish these frauds, they — the traders and landed money people — established United States Land Office Registras and Receivers. (These are but a few of the many instances of the debauching of every legislature in the United States).

The working class has allowed itself to be duped; they allowed false issues to divide them; they made no concerted effort to gain the strategic standpoint — governmental power.

The British Crown had its subjects control the Indian Department. Many of the King's subjects held commissions under the British Government and led the Indians, during the late war of 1812-1815, in an underhanded manner.

What more proof is needed to substantiate the Treaties between the monied landed people calling themselves the United States and the Crown that controls us today? One more point confirms that the first Bank of the United States was private:

> The trading class [the law-merchant people] demanded State-created banks having the power to issue money. As the courts invariably responded to the interests and decrees of the dominant class, it was quickly decided that "bills of Credit" was not meant to cover "bank notes." This was a new and surprising construction; but judicial decision and precedent made it virtually a law more binding than any constitutional insertion. The charted monopoly held by the merchants who controlled the United States Bank was not accepted passively by others of the commercial class.

Consider now *A History of the American Bar, 1966,* by Charles Warren:

Bar means attorney; Bar Association means *many* attorneys; Attorney General means an officer of the Common Law Courts; Solicitor General means an officer of the Courts of Chancery.

Warren's book shows how the American Bar was devised, and that it is part of the English Bar under the King. It would have to be so, due to the Treaty between the United States and the Crown.

In reading that book, without the information presented here, you would not see how we are controlled; to what common law they refer; and many other things that will lead to our destruction.

> Most men are allured to the trade of law, grounding their purposes not on the prudent and heavenly contemplation of justice and equity which was never taught them, but on the promise and pleasing thoughts of litigious terms, fat contentions and flowing fees. — *John Milton*

Discourse on the Rise and Power of Parliament & In The Colonies, 1677, published in England.

> There was law before there was lawyers; there was a time when the common customs of the land were sufficient to secure *meum* and *tuum*. What has made it since so difficult? Nothing but the comments of lawyers confounding the text and withering the laws, to what figure best serves their purpose.

As to the common law that you "patriots" want, which is it? The common law of the Lord, or the common law of

England? The colonists never recognized the English common law as binding *ipso facto*. The common law was neither popular nor a source of pride at that time, even in England. — *Commonwealth v. Knowlton, 2 Mass. p.354 (1807).*

Quoting John Adams, 1774:

> How then do we New Englanders derive our laws, I say not from Parliament, nor from the common law; but from the law of nature and the compact made with the King in our charter. Our ancestors were entitled to the common law of England when they emigrated; as much of it as they pleased to adopt and no more. They were not bound or obliged to submit to it unless they chose to submit.

Isn't this interesting, because Spooner said Nature's or God's Law is what man is to abide by, not the common law of England. Now note the "compact" mentioned. This is the Treaty with the King that James Montgomery brought forth. Again note the word "choice." This is the "consent" that we talk about that is so critical to their gaining jurisdiction over you. See what you pick up from learning of the foundation they used to bring you under their control, and from the first few pages of Warren's book.

> Robert Quary reported to the British Board of Trade that the people in America were very turbulent and were writing their own laws, and no law of England would be used in their government till made so by an act of their own. The Colony of Connecticut's agent in London was told to argue that English common law could be binding beyond the sea only in case it had been accepted by the colonists' own choice. [Here is voluntary consent

again.] As the Bar associations grew in Connecticut and became familiar with the law of England, the legal character of the bench improved, and the rules of the common law of England became, by judicial application, the law of Connecticut. In 1779 Rhode Island adopted the English common law.

What a blessing this book has been because it shows that the Admiralty jurisdiction of the courts extended inland under the English common law, much to the dismay of those who say Admiralty is not the major player in modern America. This proves that all revenue laws are maritime based in admiralty court jurisdictions. And the lawyers are to blame. Quoting Warren, he states:

> So when the War of the Revolution broke out, the lawyer, from being an object of contempt to restrain, for whom restrictive legislation was yearly necessary during the 17th century, had become the leading man in every town in the country, taking rank with the parish clergyman and the family doctor.

Now tell me, what better way for the Crown to enforce its treaty than by having titles of nobility, esquires, in a position as law-merchants to create the legislation needed to protect the treaty? That is why the original 13th Amendment — forbidding titles of nobility for government servants — was destroyed during the War of 1912, so the esquires could exist in the court system of the trader merchants. Without these esquires the Crown could no longer function and the treaty would have been broken. These agents destroyed the principles of nature's law, the Lord's Law, that the colonists put into effect in "the General laws and the Liberties of New Plymouth Colony" which provided that:

Let The Truth Be Known

> No person shall be endamaged in respect of life, limb, liberty, good name or estate under color of law or countenance of authority, but by virtue of equity of some express law of the general court of this colony, the known law of God, or the good and equitable laws of our nation suitable to us. — *This is part of their Liberty Number I.*

In 1646 the general court itself (see *Winthrop's History of New England,* Vol. II) said:

> The laws of the colony are not diametrically opposed to the laws of England, for then they must be contrary to the laws of God on which the common law, so far as it is law, is also founded. Anything that is otherwise established is not law but error.

This, dear reader, is God's common Law that you should be striving to bring back. As Bastiat said:

> Away with their artificial systems! Away with the whims of governmental administrators, their socialized projects, their centralization, their government schools, their state religions, their tariffs, their free credit, their bank monopolies, their regulation, their restrictions, their equalization by taxation, and their pious moralization. Now that the legislators and do-gooders have so futilely inflicted so many systems upon society, may they finally end where they should have begun: May they reject all systems, and try liberty; for all liberty is an acknowledgment of faith in God and His works.

Another point to shows that without understanding, people

will gloss over key points as not being applicable to them.

Many people have read Congressman McFadden's speech in 1934 when he was trying to impeach President Roosevelt for his "crime: against the people of America" when the Federal Reserve called in the loan against the United States and took control of the United States. What the people did not read, or rather understand, as not deemed important, is the following statement McFadden made before Congress:

> Mr. Chairman, the United States is bankrupt; it has been bankrupted by the corrupt and dishonest Fed. It has repudiated its debts to its own citizens. Its chief foreign creditor is Great Britain, and a British bailiff has been at the White House, and British Agents are in the United States Treasury making inventory and arranging terms of liquidation. Mr. Chairman, the Fed has offered to collect the British claims in full force from the American public by trickery and corruption. As soon as the Hoover Moratorium was announced, Great Britain moved to consolidate her gains. After the treacherous signing away of American rights at the Seven Power Conference at London in July, 1931, which put the Fed under the control of the Bank of International Settlements, Great Britain began to tighten the hangman's noose around the neck of the United States.

Could it be that McFadden knew of the Treaty ruling America and this was his way of exposing it for fear he would be labeled a nut case by the spin doctors of government if he directly said, "look dummies, the King owned you when you joined the corporation as a citizen by the treaty the previous office holders made with him", didn't he know this?

You now know that Great Britain was just exercising its rights under the Treaties of 1606, 1782, and 1792 to further collect the perpetual debt the Congress (the Founding Fathers) had agreed to, to protect their assets in 1787. In 1933 the Crown moved to collect; seeing its take being dwindled by the corruption in Congress and the Sates, that was draining away the payments of his claims. Warren states in his book, p.247, that;

> During these first eleven years, the Court decided only 55 cases; but two of these cases were of the highest importance. *Chisholm v. Georgia,* and *Ware v. Hylton,* the famous British Debts case of 1796 which involved a question of immense pecuniary importance; namely, whether the State laws confiscating and sequestering debts due a hostile enemy, or allowing their payment in depreciated money, were valid against the provisions of the Treaty with England.

Now you know why the esquires brought English common law back into American courts that the little people hated. Warren states;

> It is probable that no one thing contributed more to inflame the public mind against the common law than did the insistence of the American courts on enforcing the harsh doctrines of the English law of criminal libel — that truth was no defense and that a jury could pass only on the fact of publication and innuendo.

Isn't that what we have today people? The courts will not listen to any truth but stand on the statutes, and will not allow your truth to prevail. The judges tell the jury that they cannot decide the law, only the facts as given to them by the esquires sitting at the King's Bench.

Warren also states, "It is a well-known fact that in its administration of justice, New Jersey has always, even to the present day [1966] followed more closely the old English precedents than any other American States."

And the government of today says that the courts of common law that the people are trying to set up are illegal? The people always have had the right to set up courts to hear claims of crimes against people's rights, and I don't mean statutory rights of citizens of a corporation called States or the United States. You will see in Warren's book on page 509 an address by an eminent lawyer of Philadelphia stating:

> American lawyers and judges adhere with professional tenacity to the laws of the Mother Country. The absolute authority of recent adjudications is disclaimed but they are received with a respect too much bordering on submission. British Commercial Law, in may respects inferior to that of the continent of Europe, is becoming the law of America. The "prize law" of Great Britain was made to be that of the United states by judicial legislation during flagrant war between the two countries.

Dear Reader, "prize law" is admiralty/maritime law, and when it comes inland it becomes known as "booty" under forfeiture laws in time of war, as under the War Powers Acts of Washington, Lincoln, and Roosevelt.

27
Finally Making Sense

Tribunals designated as District Courts of the United States are International tribunals for the IMF (the International Monetary Fund), while United States District Courts are U.S. Courts limited to the jurisdictions of Arbitration and Prize. They are all private commercial/maritime contract courts. Not one is a court designed to protect your unalienable Rights the way you believe them to be.

For example:

- US citizens cannot use District Courts to sue state Citizens.
- Territorial jurisdiction is Legislative.
- Man is not a party to the Constitution, only the States.
- The US Constitution was not provided for the inhabitants of the States, and the 5th Amendment does not apply to them, only to US citizens.
- The Federal Rules of Civil Procedure, Title 28, is an admiralty rule book.
- Liens are *in rem* actions, and statute remedy is admiralty; all contracts with government are maritime.
- The original States were all operating in vice-admiralty. All their courts were admiralty courts and the only common law remedy was through admiralty courts which we still have to this day.

Nothing has changed except that when the United States Constitution was devised all the States gave up the right to adjudicate crimes on the high seas but still retained the maritime aspect, and could rule on federal admiralty claims. The "Law of the Land" in this country is Admiralty Law, which is contract treaty law.

Let The Truth Be Known

That's right, the United States is the only country to have Admiralty as its "Law of the Land."

You have been had, and fed false information all your life and never knew it. But you do know something is wrong when you have no rights. Until 1857, admiralty was not considered inland and all courts ruled as such, but *Thomas Jackson v. Magnolia,* and *The Propeller Genesee v. Henry Fitzhugh,* overturned the *Steamboat Thomas Jefferson* which was an embarrassment to the United States. Since 1857 courts have applied admiralty to everybody in this land.

All "revenue" causes are maritime in nature, and can be found in *Benedict on Admiralty, 6th or 7th Eds,* published by Matthew P. Bender. I don't believe many of you will be buying it at a price of $2,395 FRNs, so go to your library and get a peek before they take it away. The best is the *1st Edition* published in 1850 which consists of 600 pages that are so easy to understand, that you won't find anywhere. Almost all commissioners in admiralty have it. You mistakenly call them judges.

Before 1933 when we were all presumed to be "enemies" of the Public Policy of Roosevelt's New Deal, you could get a common law remedy under 28 USC 1333 (1) from these admiralty courts, and this can be found in *The Moses Taylor, 4 Wall 411 and Knapp Stout & Co. Company v. McCaffery, 178 Ill. 107,52 N.E. 898.* But your remedy would only offset their claim; you could not get damages. If you wanted damages you would cross libel and the admiralty court might then award damages.

By the way, 42 USC 1983 is an admiralty remedy.

Admiralty, which rules this country, is the only place from which you might get damages, as the common law never gives damages.

People, you have a lot of prejudice to overcome, and misinformation. So now you know you are dealing in maritime when pursued by any taxing agency and even by the Motor Vehicle Law. If you read *Propeller Genesee* you will see what I mean. Knowing Title 26 is maritime, look at the following without rose colored glasses.

Commerce of the ATF also falls under maritime as it is a "revenue" cause of action.

You became a "taxpayer" when using the US Mails because you purchase tax stamps (called postage stamps) and affix them to the envelope just the same as the alcohol or tobacco stamp is affixed on those products, but it doesn't make you a "taxpayer" for any income tax. There is no such thing as a "1040" kind of tax. Check the validity of any assessment or summons document, see *Brafman v. US 384 F.2d 863*.

Letters or admissions containing the expression, "Without Prejudice" are not admitted as "evidence." Watch out how you use the term "Without Prejudice." Don't use the term when demanding anything, and only when forced, that way it can't be used as "evidence" in court.

You are responsible to pay the Kings Debt by Treaty when joining the corporate State of "so an so" and claiming citizenship. These cases not only pertain to the corporations called States and the United States.

The courts said you are estopped from claiming that you are not required to pay taxes, by the simple fact that you claim citizenship, as a shareholder in a joint-venture pleading, pledging to protect the corporate by-laws under the Treaty Compact with Great Britain by allowing your labor to be used as credit by the debtor Congress.

Don't you just love the corporate Constitution you would give your life to protect? What a humbug!

Our problem today is two fold.

Problem One: Recognize that we have been misled from the day we were born to revere an admiralty commerce document (the Constitution) and to believe that the Bill of Rights would protect us. This quote is from a mayor of a big city, *who is as unaware,* to a friend I know, when he wrote about Christian principles.

> The whole structure of our government was founded upon Christian principles, but unfortunately those principles have vanished in government, for the most part.

However, what's true is true. This government was not set up upon Christian Principles. It was set up under commercial principles of admiralty jurisdiction in compact with the Crown, with the Bill of Rights forced upon the corrupt Founding Fathers, to attempt to protect the people from the commercial corporation called The United States and The States.

The Constitution was not designed for the people, but only for the commercial States. In order for people to seek operative constitutional parameters they must become associated members of the State (citizens). Then the officials may, *at the discretion of the officers of the State,* grant you or decide if you deserve any relief (granted privileges can be taken away). The Constitution does not apply to people, only to the States and their officers and employees.

Problem Two: (our main problem today, tied to the first problem, because in admiralty there exists "prize law") "Prize law" is what we are dealing with in the courts of today. But this can be good, if understood.

The IRS seems never to have information about your affairs and asks you to bring all your records with you. It is never an equal fight in court. They always win, except for a small loss here and there.

THIS IS "PRIZE LAW"

You (being a "vessel of the United States") (18 USC 9) are under maritime jurisdiction (18 USC 7) and are presumed to be an enemy of the State. You have no property rights and are subject to "capture prize law."

A prize law case is not a contest between two equally matched parties contending over some quarrel or cause.

A prize law case is a process in which an <u>officer</u> of one state claims the right to seize the property of a <u>citizen</u> of another state under a friendly flag.

Therefore the officer is required to prove his claim, But he's not allowed to present evidence of his own. He needs the defendant's records and books since he has no evidence against the defendant himself.

This is not yet a criminal prosecution.

No contest exists to be won.

No attack exists to be opposed.

The officer has no evidence of his own.

No evidence supports his claim until it is provided by the party addressed.

So are you going to give the officer the admissions (the evidence) he needs? Don't. His evidence is never allowed.

However this fact is concealed from the accused.

The accused unknowingly provides the evidence and convicts himself.

This author does not imply that the reader is by any means "stupid" — only unaware. He becomes "stupid" only if when told the truth he doesn't believe it.

This author has been unaware for many decades.

Even after being made aware, I have not applied some facets of what I have learned, because the possibilities are so great. I argued one point wrongly once, by entering an affidavit that was right on point. The officials will sometimes lie to lead you off point if you don't watch out. They will latch onto one bad point, disregarding the good points, *to your demise.*

The simple lesson is, do not argue their points or their codes. When you argue you are declaring that if they did what you said they didn't do, you consent to being subject to and guilty of their charge.

The object of this book is to get you to think for yourself and understand how all this got started in the first place, and to realize that you don't have to be extorted anymore.

The corporate State's goal is to make everyone their subject so they may control every aspect of your life, and take away the rights God gave you to be free from the subjection of man's will.

Three questions remain:

"Are you a servant of the Lord who gave you your unalienable Rights? Or "are you a citizen of the State of 'so and so' who gave you statutory privileges that can be changed at the State's whim?

Last question.

"What are you going to do about it after becoming more aware? Agree? then put the book on the shelf to gather dust. This information is nice to know but what can I do about it? I'll wait and see what other people do. I'm afraid to lose what I have if I rock the boat.

Note the words of the Lord to all men:

"God's people are destroyed for lack of knowledge."
— *Hosea 4:6.*

In 1765, the Lt. Gov. Golden of New York made a statement that runs true today:

If the law profession stays united as they are now, the skills of an upright judge will never be sufficient to restrain lawyers without the security of an appeal to a common law court where they have no undo influence. Lawyers influence every branch of our government. The domination of lawyers is as destructive of Justice as is the domination of priests; both of them founded on delusion.

Alexander De Tocqueville said, "the lawyer is our national aristocracy," and rightly so. The judicial system is made up of lawyers who install their brothers to the Bench, and control the American people today.

Citizens of the State:

We don't want to be controlled by the People who legally plunder you and me. We want "freedom of choice" to govern ourselves under our Lord (our King) by whatever name He is known and called.

28
A Closing Note

in-di-ge-nous. native, inborn, natural.
ab-ro-gates. annuls.
sur-ro-gates. substitutes, replacements.

The United Nations Charter and its founding documents are patterned after the Russian Constitution of the former Soviet Union which abrogates (annuls) all constitutional "rights" by enforceable appended provisions, i.e. attached clauses.

The Soviet Constitution had a clear provision for freedom of religion, however it also included an attached clause that allowed any provision to be abrogated (annulled), when desired, by the Soviet penal code.

Under this attached clause, to the Soviet penal code, parents who tried to teach religion to their children were subject to life imprisonment; many Soviet citizens spent their lives in prison under this rule.

The U.N. Charter, therefore, has no meaning, it is a fraud.

The United Nations is the perfect government for socialists, fascists and collectivists. The people have no rights. It is a government of the government, by the government, and for only the government. It is a process whereby surrogates support the power of surrogates who work together to create, maintain and support the ultimate surrogate (substitute): a Global Government.

The Global Government has no connection with or responsibility to the people. The result is the abrogation (annulment) of the indigenous (inborn) power of mankind.

Let The Truth Be Known

The United States also has no Constitution founded on the principles of the People's indigenous (inborn) power.

The 14th Amendment to the Constitution is also patterned after the Russian Constitution of the former Soviet Union which abrogates (annuls) all constitutional "rights" by *one enforceable appended provision, i.e. attached clause.*

The First Article of the Bill of Rights is a clear provision for freedom of *religion,* freedom of *speech,* freedom of *assembly,* and freedom of the *press,* however the 14th Amendment (to the U.S. Constitution) includes an attached clause that allows any provision of the Bill of Rights to be abrogated (annulled) by the United States penal code, when desired.

We speak of the phrase in **Sect. 2 of the 14th Amendment:**

"except for rebellion ... or other crime."

This is saying that Rebellion is a crime!

re·bel·lion. 1. Open resistance or opposition to an authority or tradition. 2. Disobedience of a legal command or summons.

President Lincoln instituted the war against the southern States when he called their constitutional right to secede from the Union, "for-good-cause-shown," a "rebellion," thereby designating the citizens of the southern States as rebels.

Under the United States penal code, if the government were to declare certain actions to be against the law, parents who teach their children about religion could be charged and prosecuted as rebels.

In other words: The United States Constitution — *like the United Nations Charter* — has no meaning. The Constitution is a fraud because it says that rebellion is a crime. This implication abrogates (annuls) the indigenous power of Americans.

29
What You Might Not Know

All the money circulating in American today has been "borrowed" into existence from the non-federal Federal Reserve Bank, by the federal government and local, community banks.

To replenish the American money supply, the federal government "sells" Bonds (*IOUs; promissory notes*) to the non-federal Federal Reserve, and We-the-People have to buy back those bonds by paying taxes to the IRS — the non-federal collection arm of the non-federal Federal Reserve Bank.

In other words, our government "borrows" money that the Federal Reserve creates out of thin air by making computer entries in the federal government's bank account from which it pays its debts.

Our government prints Bonds (*IOUs; promissory notes*) that it gives as collateral to the Federal Reserve to obtain the "use" of money the Federal Reserve creates out of nothing but debt.

Other banks, businesses and investors borrow from the Federal Reserve as well, to obtain the funds that they need. They too give promissory notes (*IOUs*) to the banks that they must later redeem.

Think of the nation's money supply as a lake created and contained by a dam. As water (*currency*) flows *into* the lake, water must flow *out* of the lake, from the dam, or the water will overflow the dam and destroy the dam, and the lake.

As the Federal Reserve adds to the money supply, by creating *new* money our of thin air (*which it sells to the government and its member banks at a profit, called "in-*

terest"), old money must be drained from the lake (*from the economy*) to keep the money supply from inflating and causing prices to increase.

In times of peace, the *new* money that the Federal Reserve creates out of thin air is offset by the *old* money that the IRS siphons off from the system (*from the money supply*).

In times of war, when the government wants to tax the people more than it can openly and above board do without complaint, it must devise *other* ways to do it; *hidden* ways that are not generally recognized and understood.

For instance, the federal government buys crude oil from the crude oil producing countries of the world, at a government inflated price, then demands a rebate (*an under-the-table kick-back*) from the oil producers of the world, which *indirectly* comes from We-the-People who pay an inflated price for gasoline at the pumps, and for the heating oil we use.

Pretty neat trick. Don't you think?

It's an "excise tax" in disguise.

30
The Dollar's Demise

An all-out rout on international markets of the beleaguered U.S. dollar began as a series of explosive claims in a British newspaper, on Tuesday, October 6, 2009.

The price of gold, off for several quarters from its all-time highs reached in March, 2008, was back above the $1,000/ounce level, driven by concerns that the Federal Reserve's inflationary activities might seriously undercut the dollar's strength.

Then the bottom fell out.

The catalyst was a brief article, "The Demise of the Dollar," by investigative journalist and longtime Middle East expert Robert Fisk, writing for *The Independent.*

Fisk revealed that a coalition of oil-producing Middle Eastern states were holding secret negotiations with the likes of France, China, Russia, Brazil, and Japan, to end the decades-old system whereby oil is bought and sold exclusively in U.S. dollars.

The plan, according to Fisk, is "to end dollar dealings for oil by moving to a basket of currencies including the Japanese yen and Chinese yuan, the euro, gold and a new, unified currency planned for nations in the Guild Cooperation Council, including Saudi Arabia, Abu Dhabi, Kuwait, and Qatar." The new regime is to be phased in over the next nine years (the article claimed), with 2018 as the target year for the dollar's final demise.

In response, the dollar began to plummet against gold, and by days end gold had reached new record highs. Throughout the week, the trend continued, with gold breaching $1,050/ounce by Friday and settling at new all-time highs by the week's end, with many predicting $2,000/ounce before very long. A few prognosticators see gold eventually soaring to $5,000/ounce, an outcome that would be calamitous, both for the dollar and for the American economy.

At the time of this writing, it appears that the U.S. dollar is (without doubt) under assault, and its demise is part of a larger plan that would lead (in the end) to a "New World Financial Order."

A LOOK BACK

Back in July 1944, delegates from all 44 Allied countries convened at the Mount Washington Hotel near Bretton Woods, New Hampshire, to plan the first global economic order. World Government was in the air in the waning months of the worst war and economic crisis the world has ever seen. The Bretton Wood Conference gave birth to an embryonic system of global financial governance, at the same time when the United Nations was being planned. The institutions that emerged from Bretton Woods — the World Bank and the International Monetary Fund being the most prominent among them — became part of the United Nations system and continue to operate today.

The delegates at Bretton Woods favored the creation of a single world currency that would be issued by a global authority — a global version of the U.S. non-federal Federal Reserve Bank or the private Bank of England — to which all local currencies would be pegged. Instead, they selected the U.S. dollar as the global reserve currency on an international gold exchange standard, meaning that dollars could be redeemed for gold, but only by international traders, and that other currencies would be convertible into the dollar.

No true global central bank was formed at that time; instead, the World Bank became the lender to developing countries, and the International Monetary Fund became a mechanism for propping up weak currencies in the Third World.

Now, with the worst economic and financial crisis since the Great Depression underway, the would-be global planners are determined to bring about the greatest revolution in global financial affairs since Bretton Woods, whereby the U.S. dollar is headed for "also-ran" status. The notion that the Gulf oil producers, China, Japan, and other countries might be preparing to end the dollar monopoly on oil over the next decade is entirely plausible.

A NEW GLOBAL CURRENCY

But if the dollar is knocked from its pedestal, what will take its place?

According to former chairman of the non-federal Federal Reserve, Paul Volker, "a global economy requires a global currency," and according to the *Washington Times*, as recently as October, 2009, China and Russia "have called for a new 'global supercurrency,' similar but larger in scale to the euro, which would replace the dollar," having potential consequences devastating to the American economy, and to the sovereignty and independence of the United States and every other nation, rich or poor, in the world.

FLAWED LOGIC

The envisioned global central bank would operate along the same lines and the Federal Reserve or any other modern national central bank: It would issue fiat currency (*money not backed by a precious commodity such as gold*), manipulate interest rates, and (*at least in theory*) "control inflation."

But all these claims are based on flawed logic. Central banks *cannot* "control inflation"; they create it. Fiat money is inherently inflationary. Keeping interest rates artificially low encourages the formation of excess money and credit which fuel boom-and-bust cycles. Under a regime of fiat money and central banking, the rich get richer and the poor get poorer.

Central banks like the Federal Reserve, holding the power to print money at will, do not hesitate to do so when their own interest are threatened. Absent a gold or other precious metal standard, there are no checks on the great power of fractional reserve banking to expand the money supply to an almost infinite degree. Modern central banking benefits none but the powerful, in the long run. A global central bank would give the United Nations the ability to fund whatever activities it wanted, freeing the global organization from dependency on the contributions of member governments. A global central bank could easily be used to finance a truly independent global military and police force, for example, to keep all countries under tyrannical control.

Rather than create a global bank and an international currency as brand new institutions (*just yet*) globalist planners are more likely to retool existing institutions to fit their purposes. For a global bank and a global currency, the framework already exists in the IMF and its Special Drawing Rights (SDRs). SDRs were created in 1969, and have been used ever since as a sort of internal accounting device, and recent suggestions for a global central bank and currency have pointed to a retooled IMF platform.

Prior to World War I, the world had a dual standard: For the wealthier countries, all currencies were on the gold standard, meaning that pounds Sterling, francs, lire, U.S. dollars, and the like, could all be redeemed at will for fixed amounts of gold if the bearer should demand such redemption. Poorer countries, used the silver standard instead, but the result was the same.

Since precious metals have invariant properties, worldwide, there was no need for international bodies to regulate currency exchange rates, since gold and silver were the global currencies to which all national monetary units were "pegged." If governments tried to issue more paper currency than could be redeemed by their available stockpile of precious, in hand, the value of that currency would automatically depreciate against other more stable currencies, and the system in effect would regulate itself.

What can be done to block the creation of a full-fledged New World Financial Order?

Simple: The United States can unilaterally return to a gold standard and nationalize or abolish the Federal Reserve System. Were the dollar to return to a gold standard, it would at once be restored to its former stature, and other major currencies in the world would be forced to follow suit. The fact that the dollar/gold exchange rate might have to be realistically set a $2,000/ounce — reflecting its gradual debasement over several generations — would be less of a concern than the fact that it would be once again anchored to the surest global financial regulator ever devised, one contrived by nature rather than by flawed human ingenuity.

A return to a gold standard will not only return America to sound money and finance, but torpedo the noxious New World Financial Order as well.

Money Comes From Debt

THE FED CREATES MONEY OUT OF THIN AIR

Incorporated in 1914, the FED has since its inception been creating money out of thin air - as debt.

This is accomplished at the stroke of a pen or a computer key with nothing more than a book entry when the members of the non-federal Federal Reserve System make loans to the government, banks, businesses, and individuals.

This money [debt] is the "money supply" called the "National Debt."

Let's examine the origin and "creation" of money under this central banking system:

"As we have advised, the Federal Reserve is currently paying the Bureau of Engraving & Printing approximately $23 dollars for each 1,000 notes printed. This includes the cost of printing, paper, ink, labor, etc. Therefore 10,000 notes of any denomination, including the $100 dollar note, costs the Federal Reserve $230 dollars. In addition, the Federal Reserve must secure a pledge of collateral [IOU] equal to the face value of the notes loaned out." — *by Willian H. Ferkler, Manager Public Affairs, Dept. of Treasure, Bureau of Engraving & Printing.*

The Federal Reserve in ordering for example $100 dollar notes into existence, sends a purchase order to the U.S. Bureau of Engraving for 10,000, $100 dollar notes at a total cost of $230 dollars to the FED. In return, the FED obtains a pledge from the federal government of collateral equal to the notes' face value of $1,000,000 (1 Million) dollars. This pledge is made to the non-federal Federal

Let The Truth Be Known

Reserve carte,l by Congress, and the collateral which Congress pledges (*mortgages*) is the land, labor and assets of the American people.

THE FED CREATES MONEY OUT OF DEBT

> "Banks create money by monetizing debt." — *I Bet You Thought, by The Federal Reserve Bank of Boston.*

> "In addition to securities (*IOU's*) the FED issues debt as money. Most people do not realize that debts are assets." — *The Two Faces Of Debt, by The Federal Reserve Bank of NY.*

So the FED thinks debts are assets! How wealthy that must make you and me feel. Judging by *that* definition, most of us should be very rich indeed.

Unlike the FED, however, most of us have no means of monetizing debt, so it doesn't really count. Consider the following to gain some appreciation for how the FED creates "money" out of thin air - from debt. The incredible thing is that it is accomplished with nothing more than book entries!

1. The FED writes a check for $1,000,000 dollars This "money" is created out of thin air with nothing more than a book entry and an authorized signature on the check. Unlike a *personal* check, there is no money on deposit with the Federal Reserve to cover the check. The FED's assets are not and cannot be used.

2. The FED gives the Securities Dealer the check and the Dealer gives the FED a Government Security Bond. The Bond is backed by the government's assets and Congress' "good faith" "pledge of credit" on behalf of the American people.

3. The Securities Dealer deposits the check for $1,000,000 dollars in his bank.

4. The Dealer's bank sends the check back to the FED for payment, whereupon the FED credits the Bank's account with $1,000,000 dollars. This is all done within the legal *jurisdiction* of the Federal Reserve.

"A Federal Reserve Note is merely and IOU. Here's how it works. When the politicians want more money, they dispatch a request to the Federal Reserve for whatever sum of "money" they desire. The Bureau of Printing and engraving then prints up bonds indenturing taxpayers to redeem their debts. The bonds are then 'sold' to the Federal Reserve. But note this unusual twist — the bonds are paid for with a check backed by nothing at all! It is just as if you were to look into your account and see a balance of, say, $412 dollars and then, hearing that government bonds were for sale, write a draft for $1,000,000,000 Billion dollars. Of course, if you did that, you would go to jail. But the bankers do not. In effect, they post the money that enables their check to clear." — *by James Dale Davidson, Director, national Taxpayers Union.*

The creation of a loan is little different when you go to your neighborhood bank. Again, the "money" that is loaned is created out of thin air, with nothing more than a book entry!

"Let us see how a bank creates a mortgage lien on a house: A man who owns a building lot and has, say, $20,000 dollars, needs an additional $75,000 dollars to build a house. If the banker finds the collateral sufficient, he may credit the man's checking account with, say, $80,000 dollars — *minus several "points" for the bank for expenses* — against which checks can be written to pay for construction. When the house is completed, it will have a thirty-year lien on it at 12 to 15% interest. After working for 30 years to liquidate the debt, the owner will have paid perhaps $300,000 dollars for something that did not cost the banker a dime, in the first place! This is the magic of 'fractional reserve banking.'" — *The Battle for the Constitution, by Dr. Martin A. Larson.*

The money supply is made up predominantly of computer book entries: some 97% of it! Only 3% is actual coin and paper currency. Without a continuous and exponentially increasing cycle of borrowing, of debt, and of refinancing, the entire system would collapse.

"If all the bank loans were paid, no one would have a bank deposit and there would not be a dollar or coin of currency left in circulation. This is a staggering thought! We are completely dependent on the commercial banks. Someone has to borrow every dollar that we have in circulation. If the banks create ample synthetic money, we are prosperous; if not, we starve. We are absolutely without a permanent money system. When one gets a complete grasp of the picture, the tragic absurdity of our hopeless position is almost incredible, but there it is. This is the most important subject intelligent persons can investigate and reflect upon. It is so important that our present civilization may collapse unless this becomes widely understood and the defects remedied very soon." — *by Robert Hemphill, former Credit manager, The Federal Reserve Bank of Atlanta, in testimony before the United States Senate.*

IT IS MATHEMATICALLY IMPOSSIBLE TO PAY OFF THE NATIONAL DEBT

"The one aim of these financiers is world control by the creation of inextinguishable debts." — *Henry Ford.*

The Federal Reserve System's banks charge usury (*interest*) on the created debt money. Obviously, the money to pay the usury on the debt must come from the same source as the debt money principle itself, but the money to pay the usury is never created! Loan repayments to banks reduce the money supply, because money is removed from circulation (*returned to the thin air that it is*) when the debt is repaid.

To keep the money supply from shrinking (*evaporating*) and to pay the interest (*usury*), more borrowing is necessary. It is mathematically impossible to pay off the total sum of debt principle plus the total sum of usury.

In a futile attempt to avoid the day of reckoning, borrowers are forced to take on increasing amounts of debt to pay not only the principal of the debt, but the onerous ever-growing usury as well. Debt escalates at an exponential rate until borrowers are forced into bankruptcy. This phenomena is not unique to government borrowing, but applies to individuals and businesses too, and is now at least five times greater than even that of the government's debt!

THE MYTH WE LIVE BY TODAY

"The reason we have a multi-trillion dollar National Debt and a multi-trillion dollar private debt is because people, the government and businesses have spent beyond their means, right? WRONG! The fact is, that our monetary system guarantees that debt must increase regardless of what the government, people,

or businesses do or do not do, whether or not they balance their budgets. Suppose I loan you 10 rare Picasso paintings, the very last in existence, with the condition that you return the 10 paintings to me plus one Picasso painting as interest. If you knew that there were only 10 in existence, you would never accept such an offer, but suppose that you are naive about the creation and circulation of Picasso paintings and you accept the terms; when repayment time comes, you only possess 10, having been unable to get the nonexistent 11th Picasso You lose your house which was pledged as collateral for that debt. A silly story you say? No one would do that! Don't be so sure. Our monetary system works the same way!"
—*The Poverty Trap; Why You Can't Save*, by Richard Walbaum (1992).

Another example: Suppose you deposit $1,000 dollars into a bank at 10% compound annual interest, which means that each year you will earn interest on the interest. In 145 years you will have over $1 billion dollars, an exponential growth of 1,000,000 times!

The moral: A small amount, held as a perpetual debt, quickly compounds to astronomical amounts. Our money supply was loaned into existence, and you don't pay back a money supply. Compound interest payments will cause this debt to rise to astronomical amounts (*it already has*).

Furthermore, just like the Picasso example above, there is always more debt than there is money to pay it back, so it can never be paid back. The best we can do is to continue to refinance it.

What we are now faced with, is a financial situation virtually identical to that which Germany faced in the early-1920's, and if we don't force Congress to rectify the matter, the whole house of paper money is going to fall down around our heads, in a few short years. History is replete with examples of nations whose governments created or permitted private central banks to control and debauch their currency. The inevitable result — depression and/or hyperinflation: the worst possible economic crisis!

The ultimate mathematical equation is complete and total bankruptcy for all but the elite few, and widespread poverty, lawlessness and anarchy — much the same environment as paved the way for Hitler to be received as the "Savior" of Germany.

When our own economy collapses, the people will clamor for just such a "Savior" and the odds are that he will be just such a dictator. *"Those who will not learn from history are doomed to repeat it."*

The Insiders have been historically responsible for crises after crises and have invariably had their man waiting in the wings with the "solution."

> "In the case of the federal government, we can print money to pay for our folly for a time. But we will just continue to debase our currency and then we'll have financial collapse. That is the road we are on today. That is the direction in which the 'humanitarians' are leading us. But there is nothing 'humanitarian' about the dictatorship that must inevitable take over as terrified people cry out for leadership. There is nothing 'humanitarian' about the loss of our freedom. That is why we must be concerned about the cancerous growth of government and its steady devouring of our citizens' productive energies. I speak of this so sensitively because I hear no one discussing this danger today. Congress does not discuss it. The press does not discuss it. Look around us, the press isn't even here! The people do not discuss it, they are

unaware of it. No *counter-force* in America is being mobilized to fight this danger. The battle is being lost, and not a shot is being fired!" — *by Congressman William E. Simon, in a speech to the House of Representatives, April 30, 1976.*

"This Act establishes the most gigantic trust on earth. When the President signs this Act (the Federal Reserve Act) into law the *invisible government* by the money power, proven to exist by the Money Trust Investigation, will be legalized. The new law will create inflation whenever the money trust's want inflation. From now on depressions will be scientifically created at will." — *by Congressman Charles A. Lindberg, Sr., at the time of the passage of the Federal Reserve Act in 1913.*

"I believe that if the people of this nation fully understood what Congress has done to them over the past 49 years, they would move on Washington, they would not wait for an election. It adds up to a preconceived plan to destroy the economic and social independence of the United States." — *by Senator George W. Malone, speaking before Congress about The Federal Reserve Bank, in 1962.*

"The best way to destroy the capitalist system is to debauch the currency." — *by Vladimir Ilyich Ulyanov, commonly referred to as "Lenin."*

Breaking News

CONFIDENTIAL SOURCES REPORT that in the next few years America as we know it today will not exist. There are just a few people on the earth today who control the world. There are people on the earth today who intentionally manipulate governments, nations, peoples and currencies, and totally control them.

War is planned in about two years, circa 2012.

The Elite plan these things in advance — they know exactly what they are doing, and they will do it exactly as they say.

War is alleged to begin in the Middle East and spread from there throughout the world.

You won't know America within two years. Within two years nearly everyone will be so poor they will be unable to resist. Almost everyone will be employed by the federal government *a la* General Motors, Chrysler and the Banks, now under government control.

What about the banks? Globalists are now taking-over five or six banks every week. They want to narrow the total number of banks down to nine or ten major banks in all.

This is vertical integration of the economy; a criminal consolidation. Globalist G-20 documents of the IMF World-Bank say as much.

Yes, war is predicted to take place in about two years.

Two-time Congressional Medal of Honor winner, Major Smedley Butler, writes in his book, *"War Is A Racket"*:

War is a racket. It always has been and it always will be. It is possibly the oldest and most profitable, and probably the most vicious

racket, where profits are reckoned in dollars and losses are reckoned in lives. Only a small inside group knows what war is all about. It is conducted for the benefit of the few at the expense of the many. Out of war a very few people make huge fortunes.

He says that before the Second World War the Elite came to him and said, **"We are going to have a coup; we're going to link up with Hitler and we want you to lead a 500,000 man army and take over the United States."** Butler played along with them until he could go to the McCormick-Dickson committee and blow the whistle.

(This is mainline history. It is *not* widely known and *not* widely taught, but it's mainline history).

Butler finally woke up, a lot of people at the Pentagon, and when the globalists told the Brass that they were going to overthrow America, a lot of the Generals refused to cooperate, and left office. There are a lot of other "Aces in the Hole" out there, like Smedley Butler.

A lot of people who we think are our friends are going to turn out to be our enemies, and a lot of people we *don't* think are our friends are going to end up being our friends.

Rand Corporation documents, and others, have stated that the Elite plan to stage another war to help build the New World Order, because a war will unify the people around the governments, to follow their orders.

The globalists will unite everything and use this as the "final straw that breaks the camel's back."

After they have escalated inflation, over the next two years, and basically destroyed the dollar because OPEC's not going to use dollars anymore, they're going to use a basket load of other currencies instead.

If you *protest* they will use the Enemy Sedition Act saying, **"we're at war: you can't protest the carbon tax, or** the "citizen-tattle-tales, etc.," and they'll stage terrorist attacks and say that foreigners are doing it; and this is their plan.

These CONFIDENTIAL SOURCES are not just some alarmist out there, these facts were revealed just days before the publication date of this book.

What the Elite refer to as their "Devil's Messiah" is not some man; or an "end-time" anti-Christ — but the system of deception that they have used over a period of years by which they have taken away America's God.

The first textbook ever used in our schools here in the United States of America, was the original *McGuffy's Reader*.

With the *McGuffy's Reader* the first schools that were ever held here in America were established for the purpose of teaching people how to read so they could read the Bible.

Listen to this brief section of the *McGuffy's Reader*:

O, my God. Do not allow me to sin. Help me to do as I am told. Let me do unto others as I would have them do unto me. Our God can see all that we do. God has an ear to all that we hear and say. Let all I do be fit for His eye.

The Elite had to remove the God of America before they could conquer the Republic.

The 1828 Webster's Dictionary was written for the purpose of preserving the language of the Scriptures so that the Bible would always have the same meaning regardless of how time might change how the people use the words.

The Elite had to take away America's God via their "Devil's Messiah," the systematic plan for what they are doing in America to remove all righteousness, decency and honesty from the government, and from the political system of the United States of America.

By evolution they have caused human beings to think that they are nothing but evolutionized animals so they will act like them. That is exactly the way many people are acting like out on the streets today.

The globalists have subverted America through the churches and the schools.

In 1964 the government came to the Pastors of the churches and said, "We would like to have you accept a 501(c)3 organizational status, so that the government can grant all of your Parishioners, who give money to your church, a tax deduction for them." They asked if the Pastors would be *willing* to have them do this; then, several years later it was required. This was a trap — a part of the plans of the Elite. They had to remove God from the churches and schools, from education, from the entire revolution, so humans would think that they are animals, not men.

We challenge you to find, **"the separation of Church and State"** anywhere in the Constitution of the United States. Tell us *anywhere* in that document where, **"the separation of Church and State"** is used.

They have federalized the churches by having them fill out dossiers on members. The Elite are attacking all the religions, but especially Christianity. If you don't owe your allegiance to God, you owe it to the State.

They are wrecking anything that they don't control via clergy response-teams.

The founders ordered the State not to get involved with the Church; to never meddle with the Church. But the Church was *expected* to be involved with the State all they wanted to. Pastors used to preach electoral sermons. They talked about the candidates. They can't do that any more today. Their hands are bound in this regard.

The First Article of the Bill of Rights says:

<u>Congress shall make no law respecting an establishment of religion</u>, <u>or prohibiting the free exercise thereof</u>; or abridging the freedom of speech or of the press; or the right of the people peaceably to assemble, and to petition the Government for a redress of grievances.

How long are you Pastors going to sit there and be pansies? Get off you duffs, Pastors. You ought to be preaching electoral sermons. You ought to be preaching on prostitution and drugs, on what is happening to our Republic, via learning and teaching courses on the Constitution, in your church. If you don't, Homeland Security has you right where they want you, under their thumb.

When they ask that you to give them information about your parishioners, know that they are going to use this information to the destruction of your parishioners whenever they get ready to do what they intend to do, two years from now. Pastors you are getting set-up; you are being used as pawns.

There is no such thing as **"the separation of Church and State."** The state ought to stay out of the Church. You have no business having a **503(c)3 non-profit "charitable trust" classification.**

You should be telling your Congressmen what to do.

War will begin in about two years. We have a maximum of two years to turn this country around. If we have not risen up and rebelled against the tyrants within the next two years, our Republic will be gone.

"If my people, which are called by my name, shall humble themselves, and pray, and seek my face, and turn from their wicked ways; then I will hear from heaven, and will forgive their sin, and will heal their land."

— 2 Chronicles 7:14.

Epilogue

Like you, the people in the government today are blindly following the Pied Piper, and have no idea of what they are doing to America . . . except for those in high places . . . and, of course, law professors and high court judges called Justices.

In Britain, the Exchequer is *their* Federal Reserve, the same as *our* Federal Reserve here in America. They call it a different name hoping that no one will catch on.

Who wrote the Federal Reserve Act and put it in place in this country? Bankers from the Bank of England and their counter parts in New York, New York.

See *A tribute to Congressman Louis Thomas McFadden*, in the Appendix, adapted from the introduction of a 500 page book on the collected Congressional speeches of Congressman McFadden, available from Emissary Publications.

These excerpts from the Congressional Record give us just a hint of the courage demonstrated by Mr. McFadden.

From these it is clear that he realized the evil nature of the beings who gained control of the government, of our elected officials, and of our monetary system, who had/have a total disregard for humnan life ... including his.

See especially the Congressional Record of June 14, 1934.

APPENDIX

A tribute to Congressman Louis Thomas McFadden

Louis Thomas McFadden was born in Troy, Bradford County, Pennsylvania **on October 1, 1876.** He attended public schools and a commercial college. At sixteen he took a job as office boy in the First National Bank in Canton, Pennsylvania, a small town near his birthplace. Seven years later he was a cashier, **and in 1916 he became the president of the bank.** Meanwhile, in 1898 he had married Helen Westgate of Canton, by whom he had three children: two sons and one daughter. **His political career began in 1914 when he was elected to Congress** as Republican representative from the 15th district. **In 1920, he was appointed chairman of the influential House committee on Banking and Currency, a position he held until 1931.**

McFadden's later career was marked by violent criticism of his party's financial policies. **Opposition to the Hoover moratorium on war debts led him to propose** to the House on 12-13-1932 **that the President be impeached. He bitterly attacked the governors of the Federal Reserve Board for "having caused the greatest depression we have ever known." Both the President and the Board,** he was convinced, **were conspiring with the "international" bankers to ruin the country.** He lost his seat to a Democrat in 1934, although two years previously he had had the support of the Republican, Democratic and Prohibition parties. **He died in 1936 while on a visit in New York City.** [Other sources say that he did not die of natural causes.]

Congressman McFadden, born in the heartland of America, a true product of its original and unadulterated self, and because of that heritage he could do no else but battle for the land which he loved. And battle he did. Armed with the courage of his convictions and the certitude of his cause he **hurled his thundering charges against those who were plundering America and drenching the world in blood with their insane greed.** McFadden refused obeisance to the high priests of Mammon, the International Bankers, for whom he reserved the full force of his attacks. **The enormity of his revealments against the Federal Reserve Board and the Federal Reserve Banks will stagger the credibility of the reader.**

Let The Truth Be Known

The din of the battle being waged by Congressman McFadden against his opponents reverberated not only in the halls of Congress but throughout the Capitol. **The dean of Washington newspapermen at that time and founder of the National Press Club, Mr. George Stimpson, when asked in later years to comment on the seriousness and magnitude of the charges being made by McFadden, replied, "It was incredible. This town went into a state of shock. We couldn't believe what we were hearing. Of course, they said right away that he had lost his mind."** "Do you think he had?", Stimpson was asked. "Oh, no," came the reply. "But it was too much, too much for one man to do".

It was too much for one man to do, and this proved his heroism. **This speaks volumes for the courage and character of Louis T. McFadden, that he made these speeches knowing that there was no support; that there would be no support.** Was it too quixotic of him? Should he have waited, quietly gathering his information until it could have been put to more practical use?

But why was there no support? We must remember that when McFadden made these speeches **we were in the darkest days of the Great Depression,** when the nation was prostrate, and in the dark night of the soul of the American people. **A sad and defeated nation, destroyed from within**, brought to its knees, **could offer no help** when McFadden opened every door, named every name, exposing every secret of the underground government.

How could any American youth fail to be moved by the spectacle of **a small town banker rising to the leadership of our Congressional Committee on Banking and Currency, and**, in that capacity, **refusing to be bought by those who buy and sell men like cattle?** Instead, he nearly brought to a halt the vast and intricate machinations of international bankers, and their sinister schemes to attain perpetual and limitless wealth at the expense of an enslaved, drugged and brainwashed population of drone workers. For twenty years he fought our fight, while we knew little or nothing of his efforts, and when he died, the record of that struggle seemingly was buried with him.

Now we bring it to light, every word faithfully reproduced from the Congressional Record, not only to enshrine his memory in our hearts, but also **to give us a standard to which we can rally.** We can no longer endure the pitiful half-men, half-women, posturing on the slave block in their efforts to present their best side to the sneering slave-dealers, and **we do not refer here to some mythical beings, but rather to** the so-called public representatives, **the men who have inherited Louis McFadden's mantle in the Congress of the United States.** These men are a poor bargain even for their masters, and even less a bargain are they for us. **Let us demand from them the heroism, the self-sacrifice, the patriotism which Louis T. McFadden gave us** without our asking for it. **And if they do not have it to give, then sweep them out.**

Do we dare to admit that everything which has happened to America since the Whiskey Rebellion has been the result of foreign influences, of alien conspiracies carried out through fetid and subterranean corridors of power, the work of the government that dares not speak its name?

The Civil War, World War I, the Great Depression, World War II... these were events which were not desired by the American people. They were not planned by the American people. They were not voluntarily entered into by the American people. But all of these events were the result of the planning of men who have no addresses, no fixed homes, no substantial loyalties save only to their own criminal interests. These are men who in healthier times were sent to the gibbet, but today we make them presidents of our banks and universities, and we watch appalled at the chaos and destruction which ensures from their every act.

Let us remember that **for ten years, Congressman McFadden had been Chairman of the House Banking and Currency Committee.** While exercising the duties of this position he exposed some of the greatest crimes of the century, **including his stinging indictment of the Board of Governors of the Federal Reserve System in which he charged them with having treasonably conspired to destroy constitutional government in the United States."**

Because of these exposures, Louis T. McFadden had unleashed the full power of the international criminals against him. When he made these speeches, he was alone. He had nothing to look forward to save his own political demise. **The power and pelf of his enemies was brought to bear, and the political life of this great servant of the people was terminated in the November 1934 elections**, held in the 15th Congressional District of Pennsylvania.

These speeches are the personal signature of a great man, a hero fighting to the death, surrounded, but never thinking of surrender, the final gesture of a man we should all honor and emulate, an American worthy of the name.

~~~~~~

Congressional Record: January 8, 1934:

Congressman McFadden: "The Congress of the United States must immediately throw the searchlight of investigation into this dark corner, or we are going to be swamped with political influences that are manufactured in foreign countries and that will lead us to the surrender of our heritage of living, just as has been done on former occasions.

Just as we did, for example, when we entered into the Jay Treaty with England, which was ratified on June 24, 1795, whereby we needlessly surrendered our right to the freedom of the seas.

We fought the War of 1812 to regain this right, but the same political influences prevented even a discussion of this subject at the treaty which terminated that war. President Wilson vowed to regain the freedom of the seas at the Treaty of Versailles; but did we regain it? Is the Jay Treaty still in force?...."

"I stand here and say to you that I have studied these records, and not only did we adopt this monetary policy without debate, not only did we adopt it without consideration but we adopted it without even knowledge of what we were doing!

It was a piece of legislative trickery; it was a piece of work in the committee that was silent and secretive. Even members of the committee did not know what was being done, according to their own declarations. The President and Members of the House did not know they were acting on such a measure. But, as I have said before, the shadow of the hand of England rests over this enactment." (C R, January 8, 1934)

~~~~~~

Congressional Record: January 8, 1934

Congressman Fiesinger: "You will recall the gentleman spoke about Professor Sprague, who was in the Treasury Department as adviser to the Treasury after he came as adviser for the Bank of England. He was also monetary adviser to the Economic Conference in London."

Congressman Fiesinger: "I was just going to remark that very thing, that the power to "coin and fix the value of money" is solely within the power of the Congress of the United States and it cannot be delegated to anybody else in the world."

Congressman McFadden: "Will the gentleman yield further?"

Congressman Fiesinger: " I do."

Congressman McFadden: "What does the gentleman say in regard to the delegation of that power to the Federal Reserve System?"

Congressman Fiesinger: "I say it is illegal. I say it is unconstitutional, as far as it affects the value of basic money. Power to control credits may be in a different class."

Congressman McFadden: "The gentleman recognizes that that was done, does he not?"

Congressman Fiesinger: "Well, I think I recognize that fact; but it may be that Congress intended to delegate banking and credit control and not the control of the basic money values."

Congressman McFadden: " The Federal Reserve System has the power to issue Federal Reserve notes, which circulate as money?"

Congressman Fiesinger: "It has. Of course, they are promises to pay. **They are credits or IOU's of the bank.**"

Congressman McFadden: "And that power was delegated by Congress in the Federal Reserve Act."

Congressman Fiesinger: "Yes, sir; with the intent to regulate the volume of credit."

Congressman McFadden: "And is being pursued by them, which gives the Federal Reserve System control over the money and credit in the United States."....

Congressman Mott: "What does the gentleman say about the delegation by Congress to the President to fix the value of money, under the farm bill?"

Congressman Fiesinger: "I think it was illegal, and the President did not want it. It was forced upon him. He never asked to have the amendment attached to the farm bill. It was forced upon him, and he is exercising the power because he was forced to exercise it; a power that he never wanted, and I say it is all illegal and unconstitutional."

Congressman McFadden: "If the gentleman has been familiar with the activities of Dr. Sprague over the history of the Federal Reserve System, he well knows that Dr. Sprague has been in all of the conferences, practically, between the Bank of England, officers of the Federal Reserve bank in New York and other central banks, which have had for their purpose the dealing with national and international price levels. That was one of the functions that he was exercising as expert adviser of the Bank of England."

Congressman Fiesinger: " Now, I understand that Dr. Sprague at the London conference was willing to peg the dollar to the British pound at $3.50, and, if he had done that, the price levels in America would have been in the control of the Bank of England, and it would have been so low it would have wrecked our national economy."

Congressman Lamneck: "Will the gentleman please insert at this point what Dr. Sprague said about who should control the price level?"

Congressman Fiesinger: "I may say-I did not expect to answer that question, but Dr. Sprague, in a conference he had, stated he believed that the value of gold should be controlled by the British, because they were more competent, from banking experience, so to do." (CR,1-8-1934)

~~~~~~~~~~~~~~~~~~~~~~~~~~~~~~

Congressional Record, January 20, 1934

Congressman McFadden: " I am quoting from the President's message to Congress on this very measure. I quote:

"That the title of all gold be in the Government. The total stock will serve as a permanent and fixed metallic

reserve which will change in amount only as far as necessary for the settlement of international balances or as may be required by future agreement among nations of the world for a redistribution of the world stock of monetary gold."

Congressman McFadden: "I say again what I have repeatedly said, that there is a definite plan for the redistribution of the gold of this country and of the world's gold. The plan has been known ever since the establishment of the Bank for International Settlements that through that medium, or one similar to it, eventually the redistribution of gold would take place." CR, 1-20-1934)

~~~~~~

Congressional Record: January 30, 1934

Congressman McFadden: "The gentleman, of course, is aware of the fact that the *Council of the Federation of Churches of Christ is an offshoot of the Carnegie Foundation which is operating in this country as a British-propaganda organization,* tied up with all of the other subversive organizations which are trying to hold down proper preparedness in the United States. [Applause] (CR, 1-30-1934

~~~~~~

Congressional Record: February 20, 1934

Congressman McFadden: "Why should the United States be buying gold and paying $35 an ounce for it? Why Should the United States be making Great Britain a present of $14.33 an ounce on the hundreds of millions of dollars of British gold that is being shipped to the United States through this process by favoring four London gold brokers?

Why should the United States set a price of $35 and pay Great Britain an increase of $14.33 on every ounce of gold? This is interesting when you consider that three fourths of all the gold produced in the world is produced in the British Empire. Did we do this because Great Britain demanded it? Is it possible that this $14.33 profit to Great Britain on every ounce of gold shipped into the United States is for settlement of a debt that the United States owes to Great Britain? (CR 2-20-1934

~~~~~~

Let The Truth Be Known

Congressional Record: March 3, 1934

Congressman Weideman: *"So the paramount issue of today is this: Shall the Government of the United States be run for the benefit of the international bankers or shall the citizens of the United States be given the right to 'life, liberty, and the pursuit of happiness'?* Shall we replace the Statue of Liberty with the golden statue erected to the god of greed? Shall we forget that the only time our Saviour used force was when he drove the money changers from the temple? Let us reestablish the principle that we all believe in: That all men are entitled to a right to work, to own their own homes, to reap a just reward for their labors, and to enjoy nature's sunshine as God intended. We owe it to our children that we shall not depart and leave them in a condition of bondage and slavery to organized greed and gold."

Congressman Lemke: "....This nation is bankrupt; every State in this Union is bankrupt; the people of the United States, as a whole, are bankrupt.

The public and private debts of this Nation, which are evidenced by bonds, mortgages, notes, or other written instruments amount to about $250,000,000,000, and it is estimated that there is *about $50,000,000,000 of which there is no record,* making in all about $300,000,000,000 of public and private debts.

The total physical cash value of all the property in the United States is now estimated at about $70,000,000,000. That is more than it would bring if sold at public auction. In this we do not include debts or the evidence of debts, such as bonds, mortgages, and so forth. These are not physical property. They will have to be paid out of the physical property.

How are we going to pay $300,000,000,000 with only $70,000,000,000?" (CR, 3-3-1934)

~~~~~~~~~~~~~~~~~~~~~~~~~~~~~~~~~~~~

Congressional Record, March 13, 1934

Congressman McFadden: "In view of what the gentleman has just said, recall that Theodore Roosevelt, the year that he passed on, made a statement to the effect that Felix Frankfurter is the most dangerous man in the United States to our form of government." (CR, 3-13-1934)

Congressional Record, March 15, 1934

Congressman McFadden: "It is right in line with the plan which is now being worked out in England. I want to point out to the House that there is a concerted movement not only in England but in the United States. In the United States this movement is in charge of certain men now engaged in writing legislation in Department of Agriculture. I refer to Mr. Tugwell, Mr. Mordecai Ezekiel, and Mr. Frank, and their immediate associates, some of whom are in other departments and some of whom are outside; and I may even go so far as to say that they are aided and abetted in this matter apparently by the Secretary of Agriculture.

Their action in this matter is also assisted and aided through the agency of the Foreign Policy Association of the United States, which is directly connected with the Fabian Society, or a branch of it, in England, which at the present time is attempting to take over the control of agriculture and its operation in England, as well as the industries therein located. I call your especial attention to the recent article, *America Must Choose*, by Secretary of Agriculture Wallace, a syndicated article put out under the auspices of the Foreign Policy Association of New York and copyrighted by them. This article is quite in keeping with the plan of the British offspring of the Fabian group.

One of the stalwarts against the move in England is Stanley Baldwin. Mr. Baldwin issued a statement which was printed in the United States recently. It was a statement made over the radio, and, if I have time, I will read it to you, because he is standing today against the movement in England that I am speaking against now, and that movement is evidenced by this legislation and any other kind of legislation following, which have for their purpose the regimenting of all production in the United States, leading up to an absolute dictatorship.

The quotation I refer to from Mr. Baldwin is as follows:

"Our freedom did not drop down like manna from heaven. It has been fought for from the beginning of our history and the blood of men has been shed to obtain it. It is the result of centuries of resistance to the power of the executive and it has brought us equal justice, trial by jury, freedom of worship, and freedom of religious and political opinion. Democracy is far the most difficult form of government because it requires for perfect functioning the participation of everybody.

"Democracy wants constant guarding, and for us to turn to a dictatorship would be an act of consummate cowardice, of surrender, of confession that our strength and courage alike had gone. It is quite true the wheels of our state coach may be creaking in heavy ground, but are you sure the wheels of the coach are not creaking in Moscow, Berlin, and Vienna, and even in the United States?

"The whole tendency of a dictatorship is to squeeze out the competent and independent man and create a hierarchy accustomed to obeying. Chaos often results when the original dictator goes. The rise of communism or fascism-both alike believe in force as a means of establishing their dictatorship — would kill everything that had been grown by our people for the last 800 or 1,000 years."

The plan in England to which I am referring is the "political economic plan", drawn up by Israel Moses Sief, the director of a chain-store enterprise in England called Marks & Spencer. This enterprise declared a dividend of 40 percent for 1933, and was enabled to do so by the fact that it has until now handled almost exclusively all imports from Soviet Russia, which has enabled this house to undersell competitors.....

The political economic plan is in operation in the British Government by the means of a tariff advisory board. This organization has gathered all data and statistics obtained by governmental and private organization in administrative, industrial, trade, social, educational, agricultural, and other circles. Air-force statistics are in their hands, as well as those of the law and medical professions. This organization or group have had access to all archives of the British Government, just as the 'brain trust' here in the United States have had access to archives of our Government departments.

Through the tariff advisory board, which was created in February of 1933, and headed by Sir George May, the control of industry and trade is being firmly established in the British Empire.

This tariff advisory board works in direct connection with the Treasury, and together with it devises the tariff policy. In this bill and the tariff bill which follows it is proposed to set up just such a board, under the direction of the President, as the tariff advisory board of England. The tariff board in England has been granted the powers of a law court and can exact under oath that all information concerning industry and trade be given it.

Iron and steel, as also cotton and industrials, in England have been ordered by the tariff advisory board to prepare and submit plans for the reorganization of their industries and warned that should they fail to do so, a plan for complete reconstruction would be imposed upon them. May I suggest to you the similarity of this plan with the N.R.A., and also suggest to you that the tariff advisory board in England has been granted default powers and can, therefore, impose its plan.

The tariff board is composed, in addition to Sir George May, of Sir Sidney Chapman, professor of economics and statistics, and Sir George Allen Powell, of the British Food Board and Food Council. And it is a well-known fact that this particular political economic group has close connection with the Foreign Policy Association in New York. I wish to quote from a letter from a correspondent of mine abroad, as follows:

> "It appears that the alleged 'brain trust' is supposed to greatly influence the present United States policy. Neither you nor I are particularly interested in what takes place in England, but what should interest us both, it seems to me, is that there is a strong possibility that certain members of the 'brain trust' around our President are undoubtedly in touch with this British organization and possibly are working to introduce a similar plan in the United States.
>
> "I understand the brain trust' is largely composed of Professor Frankfurter, Professor Moley, Professor Tugwell, Adolph Berle, William C. Bullitt and the mysterious Mordecai Ezekiel.
>
> "I think there is no doubt that these men all belong to this particular organization with distinct Bolshevik tendencies. So it is quite possible that should this political economic plan be developed in the United States, if this alleged 'brain trust' has really a serious influence over the judgment of our President, this plan may be attempted in our country."

Need I point out to you, who have been observing the activities of the so-called 'brain trust' in the writing and sending to the Congress of legislation, that this legislation has for its purpose the virtual setting up in the United States of a plan similar to that which is being worked out in England. I am assured by serious people who are in a position to know that this organization practically controls the British Government, and it is the opinion of those who do know that this highly organized and well-financed movement is intended to practically Sovietize the English-speaking race. I wish to quote again from my correspondent, as follows:

> Some two months ago when Israel Moses Sieff, the present head of this organization, was urged to show more activity by the members of his committee, he said, "Let us go slowly for a while and wait until we see how our plan carries out in America." (CR, 3-15-1934)

~~~~~~~~~~~~~~~~~~~~~~~~~~~~

Congressional Record, April 9, 1934

Congressman Patman: "....A Federal Reserve bank has a great privilege. It has the right to issue a blanket mortgage on all the property of all the people of this country. It is called a Federal Reserve note.

For that privilege section 16 of the act provides that when the Government prints a Federal Reserve note and guarantees to pay that note and delivers it to a Federal Reserve bank, that Federal Reserve bank shall pay — it seems to be mandatory — the rate of interest that is set by the Federal Reserve Board.

The law has never been put into effect. The Federal Reserve Board sets the zero rate. Instead of charging an interest rate which the law says they shall charge, they set no rate at all. Therefore, for the use of this great Government credit, these blanket mortgages that are issued against all the property of all the people of this Nation and against the incomes of all the people of this Nation, they do not pay one penny.

Not one penny of the stock of the Federal Reserve banks is owned by the Government or the people, but it is owned by private banks exclusively. They do not pay one penny for the use of that great privilege, to the people or to the Government. (CR, 4-9-1934)

Congressional Record, June 14, 1934 Congressman McFadden: I hope that is the case, but I may say to the gentleman that *during the sessions of this Economic Conference in London there is another meeting taking place in London.* We were advised by reports from London last Sunday of the arrival of George L. Harrison, Governor of the Federal Reserve Bank of New York, and we were advised that accompanying him was Mr. Crane, the Deputy Governor, and James P. Warburg, of the Kuhn-Loeb banking family, of New York and Hamburg, Germany, and also Mr. O. M. W. Sprague, recently in the pay of Great Britain as chief economic and financial adviser of Mr. Norman, Governor of the Bank Of England, and now supposed to represent our Treasury.

These men landed in England and rushed to the Bank of England for private conference, taking their luggage with them, before even going to their hotel. We know this conference has been taking place for the past 3 days behind closed doors in the Bank of England with these gentlemen meeting with heads of the Bank of England and the Bank for International Settlements, of Basel, Switzerland, and the head of the Bank of France, Mr. Maret. They are discussing war debts; they are discussing stabilization of exchanges and the Federal Reserve System, I may say to the Members of the House.

The Federal reserve System, headed by George L. Harrison, is our premier, who is dealing with debts behind the closed doors of the Bank of England; and the United States Treasury is there, represented by O. M. W. Sprague, who until the last 10 days was the representative of the Bank of England, and by Mr. James P. Warburg, who is the son of the principal author of the federal Reserve Act. Many things are being settled behind the closed doors of the Bank of England by this group.

No doubt this group were pleased to hear that yesterday the Congress passed amendments to the Federal Reserve Act and that the President signed the bill which turns over to the Federal Reserve System the complete total financial resources of money and credit in the United States. Apparently the domination and control of the international banking group is being strengthened....

We are being led by the international Jews operating through Great Britain and the Bank of England, and it is the purpose of those who are directing and cooperating that debts be reduced to 10 percent or canceled entirely....

Then there is James P. Warburg, who was called in by the President and who has sat in on all of the conferences here in Washington participated in by the foreign representatives recently, and he is the financial adviser at the Economic Conference and at the conferences in the Bank of England to which I have referred. Mr. Warburg, you undoubtedly know, is the head of the international Jewish financial group who were largely responsible for the loaning abroad of the vast billions of dollars by the people of the United States and which loans are now frozen.

We must not overlook the fact, however, that J. P. Morgan & Co. were close seconds in these transactions, and in connection with this I wish to point out that George L. Harrison, Governor of the Federal Reserve Bank of New York, is closely identified with the Morgan House in all of the undertakings internationally in which the Federal Reserve banks participated. (CR-6-14-1934)

Congressional Record, June 14, 1934

Congressman McFadden: "....Whereas the lobbying activities of the said British Ambassador, Sir Ronald Lindsay, carried on in the halls of the Capitol, at the British Embassy, in the houses of citizens of the United States, in the offices of predatory international bankers, on shipboard, on the trains, and elsewhere, have for their purpose the taking from the United States Treasury of assets which it is the sworn duty of this Government to protect by every means within its power, not stopping short of war, if need be; and whereas the said Lindsay's lobbying activities likewise have for their purpose the defeat of measures enacted into law by the Government of the United States to insure the repayment of moneys advanced to Great Britain on her written promise to repay them; and whereas the lobbying activities of Sir Ronald Lindsay likewise have for their object the overthrow of the Government of the United States and its reorganization as a part of the British Empire:.... (CR, 6-14-1934

Congressional Record: June 15, 1934 Congressman McFadden: "At that time a man named Jacob Schiff came to this country as the agent of certain foreign money lenders. His mission was to get control of American railroads. This man was a Jew. He was the son of a rabbi. He was born in one of the Rothschilds's houses in Frankfort, Germany. He was a small fellow with a pleasant face and, if I remember correctly, his eyes were blue. At an early age he set out from Frankfort to seek his fortune and went to Hamburg, Germany. At Hamburg he entered the Warburg banking establishment. The Warburgs of Hamburg are bankers of long standing, with branches in Amsterdam and Sweden.....

Sometime before Schiff's arrival there was a firm of Jewish peddlers or merchants in Lafayette, Ind., by the name of Kuhn & Loeb. I think they were there about 1850. Probably they made money out of the new settlers who passed through Indiana on their way to the Northwest. This firm of Jews had finally moved to New York and had set themselves up as private bankers and had grown rich.

Jacob Schiff married Teresa Loeb and became the head of Kuhn, Loeb & Co. Schiff made a great deal of money here for himself and for the Jewish money lenders of London. He began to give orders to Presidents almost as a matter of course. He appears to have been a man who would stop at nothing to gain his own ends. I do not blame him for being a Jew. I blame him for being a trouble maker.

Russia had a powerful enemy in this man, Jacob Schiff. The people of the United States were led to believe that this enmity of his was caused by wrongs done to Russian Jews. I look elsewhere for the motives which animated him. In the 1890's Schiff was the agent in this country of Ernest Cassell and other London money lenders. These money lenders were looking forward to a war between England and Russia and were making preparations for propaganda designed to support England in the United States.

This country was then a debtor nation, paying a high yearly tribute to Schiff and his principals. Schiff accordingly took it upon himself to create a prejudice in the United States against Russia. He did this by presenting the supposed wrongs of the Russian Jews to the American public. Unpleasant tales began to appear in print. School children in this country were told the Jewish children were crippled for life by Russian soldiers wielding the knout. By unfair means a wedge was driven between Russia and the United States.

One of Schiff's schemes was a sort of wholesale importation of Russian Jews into the United States. He drew up divers and sundry regulations for the temporary transplantation of these Jewish emigrants. He would not, he said, have them enter this country through the port of New York, because they might like New York too well to leave it for the outposts he had selected for them. He said it would be best to have them come in at New Orleans and to have them stay there two weeks, "so that they could pick up a few words of English and get a little money" before setting off for what he called the "American hinterland."

How they were to get the money he did not say. Aided by Schiff and his associates, many Russian Jews came to this country about that time and were naturalized here. A number of these naturalized Jews then returned to Russia. Upon their return to that country, they immediately claimed exemption there from the regulations of domicile imposed on Jews; that is, they claimed the right to live on purely Russian soil because they were American citizens, or "Yankee" Jews.

Disorders occurred and were exploited in the American press. Riots and bombings and assassinations, for which somebody furnished money, took place. The perpetrators of these outrages appear to have been shielded by powerful financial interests. While this was going on in Russia, a shameless campaign of lying was conducted here, and large sums of money were spent to make the general American public believe that the Jews in Russia were a simple and guileless folk ground down by the Russians and needing the protection of the great benefactor, of all the world-Uncle Sam.

In other words, we were deceived. We were so deceived that we allowed them to come in here and to take the bread out of the mouths of our own American citizens. I come now to the time when war was declared between Russia and Japan. This was bought about by a skillful use of Japan so that England would not have to fight Russia in India. It was cheaper and more convenient for England to have Japan fight Russia than to do it herself.

As was to be expected, Schiff and his London associates financed Japan. They drew immense quantities of money out of the United States for that purpose. The background for the loans they floated in this country had been skillfully prepared. The "sob stuff", of which Schiff was a master, had sunk into the hearts of sympathetic Americans. The loans were a great success. Millions of American dollars were sent to Japan by Schiff and his London associates. England's stranglehold on India was made secure. Russia was prevented form entering the Khyber Pass and falling on India from the northwest. Japan at the same time was built up and became a great world power, and as such is now facing us in the Pacific.

All this was accomplished by control of the organs of American publicity, releases to the effect that Russian Jews and "Yankee" Jews were being persecuted in Russia, and by the selling of Japanese war bonds to American citizens. While the Russo-Japanese War was in progress President Theodore Roosevelt offered to act as peacemaker, and a conference between representatives of the billigerents was arranged to take place at Portsmouth, N.H. When the Portsmouth Conference took place, Jacob Schiff attended it and used such influence as he had with Theodore Roosevelt to win favors for Japan at the expense of Russia.

His main object, then as always, was humiliation of Russians, whose only crime was that they were Russians and not Jews. He endeavored to humiliate the Russians, but Count Witte, the Russian plenipotentiary, did not allow him to succeed in this attempt. Schiff's power and the power of his organized propaganda were well understood by Count Witte, however. Consequently he was not surprised when President Roosevelt, who was often deceived, twice asked him to have Russia treat Russian Jews who had become naturalized in the United States and who had thereafter returned to live in Russia with special consideration; that is, not as Jews but as Americans.

Witte carried home a letter from Roosevelt embodying this plea. Mr. Speaker, the restrictions upon Jews in Russia at that time may or may not have been onerous. But onerous or not, before the Russians had time to change them, Schiff had the 80-year-old-treaty of friendship and good will between Russia and the United States denounced. Speaking of this matter, Count Witte says in his autobiography: "The Russians lost the friendship of the American people."

Mr. Speaker, I cannot believe that those people — the real Russians — ever lost the true friendship of the American people. They were done away with to suit the ambitions of those who intend to be the financial masters of the world, and some of us were deceived into thinking that in some mysterious way they, themselves, were to blame. The chasm that suddenly opened between ourselves and our old friends and well-wishers in Russia was a chasm created by Schiff the vindic-

Let The Truth Be Known

tive in his inhuman greed, and he created it in the name of the Jewish religion....

Mr. Speaker, the people of the United States should not permit financial interests or any other special interests to dictate the foreign policy of the United States Government. But in this connection history is now repeating itself. You have heard, no doubt, of the so-called persecutions of Jews in Germany. Mr. Speaker, there is no real persecution of Jews in Germany. Hitler and the Warburgs, the Mendelssohns and the Rothschilds, appear to be on the best of terms.

There is no real persecution of the Jews in Germany, but there has been a pretended persecution of them because there are 200,000 unwanted Communistic Jews in Germany, largely Galician Jews who entered Germany after the World War, and Germany is very anxious to get rid of those particular Communistic Jews. The Germans wish to preserve the purity of their own blond racial stock. They are willing to keep rich Jews like Max Warburg and Franz Mendelssohns, whose families have lived in Germany so long that they have acquired some German national characteristics. But the Germans are not willing to keep the Galician Jews, the Upstarts.

So a great show is put on, largely by German Jews themselves, in the hope that Uncle Sam will prove himself to be as foolish as he was before and that we will allow those Galician and Communistic Jews to come in here. That is why Miss Perking has been placed in charge of the Department of Labor. She is there to lower the immigration bars. It is thought that, being a woman, she may disarm criticism. She is and old hand with the international Jewish bankers. If she were not, she would not be here in a Jewish-controlled administration.

When the so-called "anti-Semitic campaign" designed for American consumption was launched in Germany, France was alarmed because she feared the Galician Jews might be dumped on French soil. French newspapers published articles concerning the menace, but now that France has been shown that the purpose of the anti-Semitic campaign is to dump the 200,000 communistic Jews on the United States she is worried no longer. "Ah", she says, "Ol' Uncle Sam, he is to be the goat. Very good."

Mr. Speaker, I regard it as a pity that there are Americans who love to fawn upon the money Jews and to flatter them. Some of these unfortunates are under obligations to Jewish money changers and dare not cross them....

You have witnessed the unlawful seizure by Franklin D. Roosevelt of gold reserves and other values belonging to the people of the United States, the destruction of banks, the attempted whitewashing of the Federal Reserve Board and Federal Reserve banks, the corruption of which he admitted in his campaign harangues; and you may have noticed that what was confiscated is not in the hands of the present constitutional Government but in the hands of the international bankers who are the nucleus of the new government Roosevelt is seeking to establish here.

Roosevelt's actions are not in accordance with the Constitution of the United States. They are in accordance with the plans of the Third International.

At one time Trotzky was a favorite with Jacob Schiff. During the war Trotzky edited *Novy Mir* and conducted mass meetings in New York. When he left the United States to return to Russia, he is said upon good authority to have traveled on Schiff's money and under Schiff's protection. He was captured by the British at Halifax and immediately, on advice from a highly placed personage, set free. Shortly after his arrival in Russia he was informed that he had credit in Sweden at the Swedish branch of the bank owned by Max Warburg, of Hamburg. This credit helped to finance the seizure of the Russian revolution by the international Jewish bankers. It assisted them in subverting it to their own ends.

At the present time the Soviet Union is in debt. From the date of Trotzky's return to Russia the course of Russian history has, indeed, been greatly affected by the operations of international bankers. They have acted through German and English institutions and have kept Russia in bondage to themselves. Their relatives in Germany have drawn immense sums of money from the United States and have in turn financed their agents in Russia at a handsome profit. The Soviet Government has been given United States Treasury funds by the Federal Reserve banks acting through the Chase Bank and the Guaranty Trust Co. and other banks in New York City.

England, no less than Germany, has drawn money from us through the Federal Reserve banks and has re-lent it at high rates of interest to the Soviet Government or has used it to finance her sales to Soviet Russia and her engineering works within the Russian boundaries.

The Dnieperstroy Dam was built with funds unlawfully taken from the United States Treasury by the corrupt and dishonest Federal Reserve Board and the Federal Reserve banks....

Mr. Speaker, an immense amount of United States money has been used abroad in preparations for war and in the acquisition and the manufacture of war supplies. Germany is said to be part owner of a large poison-gas factory at Troitsk on Russian soil. China is almost completely Sovietized, and in the Asiatic interior huge stocks of munitions are said to be stored awaiting the day when the war lords of the United States will ship United States troops to Asia.

Mr. Speaker, the United States should look before it leaps into another war, especially a war in Asia. It should decide whether it is worth while to join hands with Russia and China in a war against Japan. For myself, I say and I have said it often that the United States should remember George Washington's advice. It should mind its own business and stay home. It should not permit the Jewish international bankers to drive it into another war so that they and their Gentile fronts and sycophants by way of Louis McHenry Howe, the graftmaster, may reap rich profits on everything an army needs from toilet kits to airplanes, submarines, tanks gas masks, poison gas, ammunition, bayonets, guns, and other paraphernalia and instruments of destruction. (CR, June 15, 1934)

~~~~~~~~~~~~~~~~~~~~~~~~~~~~~

OTHER WORKS
BY THE AUTHOR

Commercial Redemption: The Hidden Truth
http://tinyurl.com/yj4otn4

Monitions of a Mountain Man: Manna, Money, & Me
http://tinyurl.com/ygtkak8

Maine Street Miracle: Saving Yourself And America
http://tinyurl.com/yg9q8mm

Epistle to the Americans I: What you don't know about the Income Tax
http://tinyurl.com/yfplutf

Epistle to the Americans II: What you don't know about American History
http://tinyurl.com/yzme458

Epistle to the Americans III: What you don't know about Money
http://tinyurl.com/yzuffbe

Witness to Truth I: the Reformation of the Church leading to the Coming of the Christ
http://tinyurl.com/yhowxjb

Witness to Truth II: The Science of the Christ outlined in the Revelation of St. John
http://tinyurl.com/yk8jblo

Witness to Truth III: the History of Civilization foretold in the Prophecies of Daniel
http://tinyurl.com/ygy8yrz

Let The Truth Be Known

Made in the USA
Lexington, KY
20 August 2010